THIS IS A WIN! WIN! STORY

LYNDON WEBERG

iUNIVERSE, INC.
NEW YORK   BLOOMINGTON

This is a win! win! story

iUniverse books may be ordered through booksellers or by contacting:

iUniverse
1663 Liberty Drive
Bloomington, IN 47403
www.iuniverse.com
1-800-Authors (1-800-288-4677)

ISBN: 978-1-4502-3275-3 (sc)
ISBN: 978-1-4502-3276-0 (ebk)

Printed in the United States of America

iUniverse rev. date: 8/17/2010

This is the compelling story of a partially blind man, a survivor of a kidney transplant, and his amazing recovery, testimony, and conversion from alcoholism and compulsive gambling.

If you are lonely, feel empty, or live with a huge hole in your chest or heart, you will enjoy this book. It will help you achieve fullness in your life.

LYNDON C. WEBERG

DEDICATED TO MY GRANDCHILDREN:

Morgan and Isaac Weberg - 2010

ACKNOWLEDGEMENTS:

Lorraine Wallin
Jane Schultz
Rose Weberg
Brian McCracken
Carolyn Griffin
David W. George
The Good News Holy Bible
The New King James Holy Bible
Sowers of the Seed, Inc.

Purpose of this book: To give encouragement and to win souls for JESUS CHRIST!

If you feel empty or you have a large hole in your chest, you must read this book to learn how to fill the vacancy in your heart. Most people try and fill that emptiness by external means such as drinking, drugs, gambling, pornography and so forth. This book will teach you how to fix the gap by internal means.

ABOUT THE AUTHOR

DR. WEBERG IS A RETIRED PROFESSOR EMERITUS FROM THE UNIVERSITY OF WISCONSIN-RIVER FALLS. HE TAUGHT MATHEMATICS, STATISTICS, AND COMPUTER SCIENCE DURING HIS 36 YEAR CAREER AT THAT UNIVERSITY.

HE HAS PERFORMED PROSTATE CANCER RESEARCH AT THE MAYO CLINIC AT ROCHESTER, MINNESOTA AND AT THE ARIZONA CANCER CENTER IN TUCSON, ARIZONA. PROFESSOR WEBERG HAS ALSO PERFORMED ALZHEIMER'S DISEASE RESEARCH AND NPC (NIEMAN'S PICK C) DISEASE RESEARCH AT THE UNIVERSITY MEDICAL CENTER IN TUCSON. HE HAS WRITTEN SEVERAL PAPERS AND BOOKS ON THESE SUBJECTS ALONG WITH WRITING A BOOK ENTITLED "MATH FOR PARENTS".

PROFESSOR WEBERG IS A BORN AGAIN AND SPIRIT FILLED CHRISTIAN WHO HAS WRITTEN HIS AUTOBIOGRAPHY FOR HIS FAMILY. ALSO HE HAS WRITTEN HIS BOOK AS A WARNING TO THE READER TO BE READY FOR THE LORD JESUS CHRIST'S RETURN AT ANY TIME NOW! THE RAPTURE IS COMING VERY SOON! BE READY!

THE WORDS OF HIS BOOK CAN PREPARE A PERSON WHO HAS NEVER KNOWN THE LORD TO HAVE A PERMANENT HOME IN HEAVEN FOR EVER AND EVER! READ THIS BOOK TO SEE HOW YOU CAN MAKE HEAVEN FOREVER AND EVER!

Contents

1. ANCESTORS AND EARLY DAYS

Amid strong winds and smashing waves against the boat, a group of Swedish immigrants journeyed toward America, toward a new start in the land of opportunity. The year was early 1868. Juhaan and Kareen Wieberg, coming from Ameas, Sweden of Niereke Hill, had made it through several months of a very hard journey. On the ship there had been much sickness and many burials at sea.

They landed at Ellis Island in New York and after being given thorough physicals they stayed for 2 weeks before traveling on a slow train to an area called Lund, Wisconsin. Once there they settled on a 160-acre homestead, located 4 miles east of Lund. Their first home was a dugout, arranged in a hillside on the property. They stayed there while building their new 3-room house.

They arrived in May of 1868 in the town of Lund where there was a grocery store, feed store and a place to buy eggs. Lund was 10 miles north of Pepin, a larger town and 5 miles from Plum City, another village. It was exactly 100 years later that I started my teaching career as an assistant professor at the University of Wisconsin-River Falls, only 60 miles north of Lund, WI.

Juhaan and Kareen had several children, and one of them was named Edward Wieberg, which later turned out to be my grandfather. Edward married Ellen Amelia Sundvall. They had six children: Francis, Myrtle, Lorraine, June (died early), Norris, and Lloyal. Lloyal (born in 1918) was my father. He married Carolyn Erdman in 1940 and they resided in Pepin. They were living there when I was born.

Aunt Lorraine gave me a lot of information about the early Wieberg family and I am thankful for her help. Later, the 'i' was omitted from the name Wieberg because when it was pronounced, the 'e' was all that sounded. Hence, the family name became Weberg, which it is to this day.

I am Lyndon Charles Weberg, and as I being the story of my life it is Memorial Day evening. With that in mind I want to say thank You to the Lord for all those who have lost spouses and children in previous wars, protecting our country. God bless those families.

My story goes this way: I was born on Mrs. Schruth's kitchen table on Lake Street, in Pepin, Wisconsin November 6, 1943. Mrs. Schruth was the midwife for most babies being born in that small town. Many of my relatives had entered life on that same kitchen table. I was Lloyal and Carolyn Weberg's first child and was born with bilateral congenital glaucoma, which was not determined until later. It was a controlling factor in my life. Glaucoma usually occurs in people over 40 years of age but I happened to be born with it.

For many years my father was a butter maker and a cheese maker for the State of Wisconsin. He had done a lot of work in the Pepin Creamery. I grew up living in an apartment over the Pepin Creamery. Later, we moved to Ellsworth, Wisconsin. I recall my mother telling me it was a bitter, cold gray day in Wisconsin when I was born, I can imagine, the frosty air, cold enough to snow but yet the ground bare of a white covering. What a contrast it is to the warm, beautiful Hawaii where I am this evening!

I remember growing up, riding my tricycle around the floor of the creamery, over the hoses. After my father finished salting the curd, he'd always reach into the vat and come up with a big handful of fresh salted curd. My friends and I would enjoy eating the "squeaky cheese." It always squeaked when we chewed it, which was a fascination for us.

The town overlooked Lake Pepin. The scenery was delightful from the window of our apartment. We would gaze out over Lake Pepin with appreciation. It's about seven miles long, and three miles wide, and on the other side is Minnesota.

I remember when I was a little older that my father and mother both were fond of fishing at Smith Lake, which was smaller but in the same area. Much to my delight, they would take me with them. On those particular evenings, we would fish for blue gills and croppies. Uncle Vince and Aunt Mabel would go with us, along with their boy, Vinnie. In the early evening we'd fish together. Usually we would catch a good mess of sunfish and croppies to have for the next day's meal, or a couple days later. Boy! It was really fun pulling in those fish when they were biting! I still remember what a great time we had!

I recall the treasures we discovered as children, up and down the tracks near Smith Lake and Lake Pepin. We would go across the tracks and down to the beach where we learned how to swim very early in our life. It was a good upbringing in a small town.

In 1949, my father got the word that he was going to be transferred to Ellsworth, Wisconsin. To get there, we had to travel up the road along Lake Pepin and then back into the interior of western Wisconsin. It was 1949, early in the spring. My dad was to be the head butter maker and cheese maker at the Ellsworth Creamery.

We were going to look for a house. It was interesting the way that my father chose the house. I remember coming into that town and it was a little bigger than Pepin, which was only about 600 or 700 people. Ellsworth was probably 1,800 or 1,900 people at that time. My Father knew where the creamery was and as he liked to walk to work, he chose a place where that was possible. A sign in the front yard said "For Sale." There was a tall, majestic pine tree in the front yard, as if standing guard to the one-story bungalow house. It was pleasant to view.

I recall, with sweet reminiscence, when we drove into the driveway for the first time and parked the car. I went inside with my dad. I noticed raspberry bushes growing way up to the back door. The house was sitting on an acre of land and had a garage in the back, and apple trees at the end of the long, narrow lot.

We knocked on the door and heard a weak voice say, "Come in". Dad opened the door and we met Mrs. Grape, an extremely plump, overweight lady sitting on a sofa. I thought the couch was well covered by the lady and I realized that she was unable to move very much. My dad asked if the house was for sale, and questioned her about some of the details. After looking around, he made the decision to buy that house from Mrs. Grape.

He paid $3,600 for the house and that became their home for the next 30 years. In my life, from about age 5 ½ to when I moved out after college, it was home for me for 17 years. I think of being in that house and its wonderful family times.

Dad had been a former carpenter with Uncle Louie on Mother's side, so he was a very handy guy. He started by clearing all the raspberry bushes and the land. He and Mother planted the whole backyard with a garden. They left an area close to the house for a yard of green grass and flowers. Behind the garage they planted a half acre of corn, raspberry bushes, pie plants (rhubarb), asparagus and cucumbers along the side; it was really very beautiful. The zinnias, gladiolus, pansies, petunias, and many other lovely flowers decorated the yard near the house. Four apple trees stretched across the back lot. The thought of that place brings happy memories to mind.

My dad remodeled the house, room by room. He started with the kitchen first because his wife, Carolyn Weberg, was an incredibly good cook. As a couple, they were close and cherished each other. He essentially remodeled the kitchen so it was workable for Mother. There, she could make meals in a neat kitchen with counter space and new cupboards. Living in that house after Dad remodeled it, was like living in a little dollhouse. The yard sloped down toward Highway 35 going out of Ellsworth in the direction of Uncle Norris' farm. I liked the house. It had an attic and a garage in the back, where Father parked his car. I think he had a 1949 Chevy at the time, or maybe it was a '38 Chevy (one of the two).

Now, it so happened that the line between the township and the village ran right through the driveway of our house. This meant that the house sat north and south, and it was on the east side of the driveway. The road ran right between our house and the neighbor's house on the west side of the drive. Mr. Melgard was his name and at the time when we moved there, I didn't think it mattered but soon, discovered it did. I was almost 6 and it was late summertime, with fall on its way. That road was the determining factor of what school I was going to for first grade. I was going to go to a one-room country school east of Ellsworth about a mile away but the neighbor kid I played with (Melgard's grandson) was going to the town school. So, all my friends were going to the town school. I did discover other friends to the east of me, like Barton Christianson and Kenny Shingledecker. Those kids went to the same country school I did. That was a story in itself.

The first day Dad took me to the country school on Highway 35, east of town about a half mile. There's a line and you take the left part of the line and it is Highway 72 that goes out about another three-quarters of a mile. On the left side of the road sat a country school named Cudd School.

The very first day, probably in August, I registered for school. It really was a surprise to me because I was just a little kid. I wasn't even six years old yet; my birthday was in November. I looked around the schoolyard and observed all sized kids sitting on the front porch and around on the side of the school. It was sort of interesting. There was an entryway where students could hang jackets and other things. We walked into the one room schoolhouse. It had windows all the way along the sides of it. It also had desks, starting with very small ones on the left side and then becoming progressively larger as they went from the left to the right with the teacher's desk up front. There was the United States flag in front, and a school bell on top of the schoolhouse.

Out in back there were two outhouses, boys' and girls'. The schoolyard was fairly large so it was a good opportunity for a lot of playground and other things as well. I was scared that first day because some of the big eighth graders looked huge to me (compared to what I was). I became braver on the second and third day.

The lady who was teaching was Mrs. Swanson, and she enrolled me in the class and explained that I was to report on one of the later days of August, to actually begin my school career at that one room country school.

I remember Mom and Dad taking me there the very first day to the school, and the small desk up toward the front that was going to be mine. There were two of us in the first grade; Carolyn Shoemaker was the other first grader. Barton Christenson started one year later. I had Mrs. Swanson for the first couple years. And then when I was in third grade Mrs. Ed Steiner came to be the teacher, and I had her from grade three to grade eight. I do remember many, many things that were outstanding in my education at the one room country school.

Mrs. Swanson had little or no discipline problem with the bigger boys. When we would be called forward, Carolyn and I would go sit in little chairs and would have a lesson about mathematics or science, or something, and then we'd go back to our seats. We'd be given our books and the next grade would come forward, and that had two or three people in it.

With Mrs. Steinier we went through the whole routine of the class, up until the eighth grade. I felt as if we were like a family because she would ask the second graders to help us understand the things we had been taught in our class. It was an exceedingly helpful approach. As time went on, I truly appreciated that education very much.

I remember saying the Pledge of Allegiance to the Flag every day when we went to school and it was definitely "Under God," so there's no lack of that in my education or in my life. I really appreciated it. I remember at recess time we would go out and we'd run around. I remember playing games in the yard at the country school, playing hide-and-seek and drop the handkerchief and ring-around-the-rosie, and all kinds of games like that.

I believe it was in first grade that it became difficult for me to see the board in front of me. My parents took me to an eye doctor, a Dr. Brucegard over at Red Wing, and it was there determined that I was born with bilateral congenital glaucoma. I had to put drops in my eyes four times a day. Pilocarpine, was the medication, and I was also given a small pair of glasses. This is something that has continued with me throughout my life. I still have glaucoma, so I have had to put up with many things in my education because of it.

I also should mention that my mother was a very, very kind lady and a good Christian. Both my parents were Christian people, and I would go to church regularly with them and learned about Jesus very early in my life.

My mother was very patient with me, especially with my glaucoma. She'd make sure to put my drops in, and the country school teacher would do it as well. And other people, with whatever I was involved with, like Boy Scouts – they'd make sure that I had my drops in every four hours so I could continue seeing.

My mother was very, very kind. She would sit me on her knee and go through the picture Bible with me, carefully showing me all the pictures of the different phases of the Bible. I remember seeing a picture of Paul going over the wall when the disciples lowered him. This was when all the Jewish people were upset with him after he'd converted from being a Jew that was persecuting the Christians to now being a newborn Christian.

I remember seeing Moses, when he was very small, lying in the basket in the bulrushes of a King's palace. I saw many things about Jesus regarding His crucifixion, and His praying at Gethsemane, and Easter Sunday morning, and so forth. I'm now 66 years old, and those pictures that my mother showed me still stand out vividly in my mind. So, it goes very much along with the Bible verse that says: "Train up a child in the way he should go and when he gets old he will not depart from his way." Yes, that had a great deal of influence on my life.

My parents also made sure that we knew our cousins and other families on both my father and mother's side. Almost weekly we would drive to Uncle Norris' farm to see our cousins: Vernon, Virgil, Elaine, Arlene, Judy and Jane, or Uncle Dewey's farm to see cousins Maxine, Lois Ann, and Laurel and Aunt Florence along with the tractors and all the farm animals. If we did not go to the farm, we would go to Pepin, WI, my birth place, to see my mom's sisters and their families. Sister Mabel and husband Vink had three children: Patty, Vinnie, and Jackie. Sister Violet and husband Louis had four children, cousins Ruth Ann, Robert, Paul, and Lowell to play with all the time. Sister Florence and husband Carl had two children, Ardell and Steve. Carl was about 6 feet 5 inches tall and weighed 140 lbs. and he was the only guy that when he crossed his legs while sitting, both of his feet would be flat on the floor! We all laughed at that and we kids called him "Stretch!" These were my mom's sisters in Pepin. Over the years we had many family picnics and days at the beach where most of us learned to swim in Lake Pepin. We played with inner tubes from Vink's station, cap guns, and watched Patty ice skate with her new skates (that she received in a red box) on the frozen pond between their house and the station. It was great fun for everybody because all the dads would go fishing, all the mom's would sit around on picnic blankets having a cool one, and all us kids would go swimming in the big lake.

In contrast, we as a family would go to the big city, St. Paul, Minnesota, to see my father's sister Myrtle and her husband Michael and our three cousins Kathyrn, Mickey, and Larry where we enjoyed many wonderful times. We went fishing and had many picnics with them. One time fishing with Michael, Mickey, my dad, and me we were fishing for bass very early in the morning on Balsam Lake in northern Wisconsin. Being from the big city, both Michael and Mickey had been practicing casting for several days before this fishing trip. All four of us were in a fishing boat on Balsam Lake and as we approached some lily pads, my dad told Mickey to cast out by the lily pads with a bass plug. Mickey slung the casting rod back over his shoulder with a large bass plug on it and caught Uncle Michael's glasses with the plug, throwing both the plug and glasses over by one of the lily pads. The glasses sunk to the bottom of the lake and a gigantic bass jumped out of the water and grabbed Mickey's plug; he had a fight on his hands for the next 20 minutes. Michael was upset with Mickey about the glasses but happy for him about the good-sized bass that he caught. All four of us caught bass that day. All I could think about most of the morning was some big ol' bass swimming around the lake with Uncle Mike' glasses on its face! Fortunately, Uncle Mike's glasses had landed in about 5 feet of water by the lily pads so we were able to fish them out with a pole and a dip net. All of us caught fish and glasses that day, so everyone was happy and filled with joy.

Aunt Myrtle was a neat aunt in many ways, baking us kids all kinds of cookies and good things to eat. She was a Registered Nurse for several companies in St. Paul. She was a wise older sister for my dad.

As I look back some 55 years later, I am thankful that my parents had such close relationships with their brothers and sisters.

2. GRADES 3 THROUGH 8 AT CUDD SCHOOL

In the first three grades, my eyes appeared extremely large and would protrude. Some of the older kids ridiculed me, calling me names like "big eyes" or "pop eye." It was humiliating, but at the same time I had to come to grips with it.

After receiving rides to the country school from Mrs. Rosine Hillman, I gained a new friend. Sometimes my parents would take me but at other times Mrs. Hillman picked me up and a couple other boys to the east of us and took us all to school. Her daughter, Linda Helgeson was poked fun at also; she and I became fairly good friends. We both chummed together because of the fact that others scoffed at us.

One incident I recall. One of the older boys set a trap for Linda and me. They planned and succeeded to terrorize Linda as she came around a corner of the school. I was about three feet behind her. She turned the corner and a hard softball flew and hit her hard in the stomach. She lay on the ground in terrible pain and I put my arms around her, attempting to console her so she would stop crying. About that time, Mrs. Swanson came around the corner on her way to the bathroom and asked me what happened. I told her and three bad boys had to stay after school and write on the blackboard 200 times each "I will not be mean to Linda again"! The next morning the three boys had to apologize to Linda in front of the whole school. I remember how angry I felt after the ball had hit Linda. She was my friend and we had something in common. But both of us got over it and continued on.

In the third grade, I had a new teacher whose name was Mrs. Katherine Steiner. She had been a Superintendent of Schools in Pierce County of Ellsworth, Wisconsin. She had become bored with her position, paperwork, and so forth and thought that coming back to the one-room country school was the answer. She did it, and took over Cudd School. It was 1951 when I entered third grade, and discovered just how much of an outstanding teacher she was. It's not that Mrs. Swanson was a bad teacher, but Mrs. Steiner seemed to be better equipped in regards to teaching all subjects. I look back now, and realize that I had a tremendous well-rounded education, as much in science and math as I did in history, art and music – I became knowledgeable in each different area. We stood every morning and recited the "Pledge of allegiance to the Flag"

Her husband Ed was a carpenter, and he had built her a Lazy Susan type of table that sat in the front of the room. Instead of a centerpiece in the Lazy Susan, there was Mrs. Steiner, on a chair in the middle of the table. Throughout the day, she would call up different classes and go through their level of teaching. She'd have flash cards for mathematics, and we'd learn the addition tables, multiplication tables, and so forth.

After lunch break, she'd gather us all around the piano and we'd sing songs for a while, and she'd read to us every day, when we came in from break or from having recess or noon hour. She would read very interesting stories like pioneer stories about the west with Buffalo Bill, Indians, "Little House on the Prairie", and other such stories. She taught us the value of reading. Sometimes Mrs. Steiner would have the older students read to the younger ones, and they would assist them in math, reading and writing skills. The whole school of 27 students was like a large family with the older children helping the younger ones to learn.

I received a library card at an early age. I'd go to the Ellsworth Public Library and check out books on Wild Bill Hickok and Buffalo Bill and all the western stories that were very much a part of my educational process at school. I really learned to love that lady a great deal; she was kind to me with my eye problem and would put eye drops in my eyes on a regular basis.

We had to carry water every day for school. Two boys were assigned per week to go to the nearby farmer in the mornings with shotgun cans to pump water out of his well and carry them back to school.

There, they'd dump them in the water cooler for the day. One week in November, I was assigned to carry water with another boy whose name was Sammy Haster. When we got to the well on that cold morning it was below freezing and I remember Sammy horsing around and getting his tongue stuck to the pump handle! He yelled because he hurt with oh, so much pain. I still remember the picture of him and his tongue stuck to the pump handle. Shortly thereafter, the farmer's wife came from the house and seeing the problem, brought out a pan of hot water to pour on the pump handle in order to free Sammy's tongue. We then carried the two shotgun cans of water back to the school and were 20 minutes late; we had to explain to Mrs. Steiner, and the whole school just howled with laughter! Sammy's tongue was very sore for a week after that morning.

To prepare for special celebrations we would rake the lawn and get all the leaves together. We would have a wiener roast, a hotdog affair with chips and everything else. On several occasions, Mrs. Steiner would pile us all in the back of her pickup and we'd go off to another country school and play a softball game. It was great and we enjoyed meeting other kids. South Rush River School was one, and Lanz School was another. I remember Lanz's ball field. It was built on a hillside so that from home base you would run down to first base, up to second, up to third, and down to home. If a ball was hit hard into the left field it would likely roll down to the center fielder and he would throw it into the infield. It was a comedy of errors all afternoon. The bases were large stones dug into the ground so when you slid into base your pants would rip and tear. The mothers of Cudd School were not very happy after a ball game because of the sewing that they had to do.

On the island of Red Wing there was also a school that we would travel to occasionally to play a ball game. It was located on the back channel of the Mississippi River and a homerun ball would fly into the River. This school would be flooded out during the spring floods.

Sometimes on Friday, Mrs. Steiner would pile us into the back of her pickup and give us a couple jars of dill pickles. We'd ride down the road to the woods where we all enjoyed a nature hike. She identified the names of flowers and leaves for us, and all the different trees. It was a beautiful time I remember well.

She had two children: a girl, Betty, and a boy, Bruce. They were in high school or entering college when she was teaching at our country school. That lady equipped me so well in my education that there was a couple of times later in life I felt the effects of her wonderful teaching in regards to making choices on which direction I would go.

But those years ago in that one room country schoolhouse, with Mrs. Steiner, were the best of times in my learning process where I was taught the blessings of education. Mrs. Steiner kept things in priority, with God first and education second. She was well rounded, thus I became well rounded. I could have majored in history, mathematics, physics, or any other subject. I reflect back on these memories many times and think how wonderful they were.

Mrs. Steiner was instrumental in getting me into the scouting program, with Cub Scouts in grade school and Boy Scouts and Explorer Scouts in High School. This culminated with my receiving the Eagle Scout Award in May of 1961. The Eagle Scout Award has been very important for me on applications and I still use all the principles in my daily living. Thank God for this wonderful program for young boys.

The humiliation of the teasing of other kids in school was devastating but yet, it was not that bad because I was so engrossed in learning. I wanted to learn everything that I possibly could from Mrs. Steiner. She was a magnificent educator who had an amazing classroom. She gave me a craving to learn, and encouragement. I realized I was capable of doing as much as any other person. She would often tell me that there would be equipment I could use in college. She instilled in me a strong desire that I could make it even if I was challenged, and a love for learning. She gave me hope! There were problems, as it was difficult for me to see a lot of things – but there was hope...

In high school I tried to play basketball and attempted to play baseball but it was difficult. I played freshman baseball and did a lot of pitching. I remember having gotten 13 strikeouts in one game. Then in my sophomore year, my vision became so poor I could not see a baseball anymore. I could not continue doing that kind of activity. I went to running track, and actually did well with it. I received a letter as a sophomore, and enjoyed it a lot.

As far as the educational process, I was a good student because of the schooling I'd received from the country school and the influence of Mrs. Steiner. I thank her to this day!

Whatever class I took in high school, whether it was U.S. history, mathematics or algebra, I was able to accomplish straight A work, thanks to her. And I thank her for that influence and help in my educational process, not only then but throughout my entire life. I believe it was because of her influence that I came to be salutatorian of the class of 1961 at Ellsworth High School. Most of the other kids who had been taught by Mr. Steiner did very well, being in the top percentages of the high school at graduation.

I also want to give tribute to some teachers at the Ellsworth High School. Mrs. Louise Rice, an English teacher was a lot like Mrs. Steiner in education priorities. Even though I could not see the black board, I was good at memorizing. I got along well with Mrs. Rice; I studied hard and she liked my memory work on conjugating verbs and pronouns and the like. She assisted me in the junior class play as "Oswald, the bug collector" and again in the senior play with Mrs. Wiberg, an English teacher, as "Attorney Van Sty" in "Ladies of the Jury". Mrs. Wiberg was another favorite of mine. She had three sons Mark, Joel, and Paul. Paul was my age so we were good friends at school and at church.

I had several mathematics courses in high school from Mr. Jack Swenson. Math came easy for me because I enjoyed solving problems, whether on paper or in life. My good memory enabled me to memorize formulas and equations easily. Not being able to see the board from the front row, I listened well and memorized everything. Mr. Swanson and one of his student teachers, Mr. Jack Dodge were great educators. There were many great educators at the Ellsworth High School, too numerous to mention here. They all helped in my obtaining a wonderful high school education in preparation for college. Thank You God, for these great teachers who touched my life!

In 1950 a baby brother was born into our family. I went to visit my Uncle Norris and Aunt Esther on their farm for about a week when he was born. They had six children, four girls named Arlene, Elaine, Judy and Jane (twins) and two boys, Virgil and Vernon.

Lyndon Weberg

I came home to the house in Ellsworth and saw my baby brother for the first time, lying on a blue blanket on the bed. His name was Ronald. He's been a very good brother to me all through my life.

One more thing – in the winter season when there was snow on the ground and it was cold, Mrs. Steiner would always have a big canister on the stove. We could bring a small jar of soup along with our bag lunches to warm up, whether it was Campbell's soup, or vegetable beef, or whatever; it tasted very, very good during the winter season. It was especially so on that type of day when it's bitterly cold outside. We used to have skating outside and make snowmen and all kinds of things – for that was life for kids back in the mid-west, for sure.

3. THE COLLEGE YEARS: HOPE

I attended college at the University of Wisconsin, River Falls (UW-RF) in 1961. Glaucoma had affected my life drastically for I was unable to do any kind of physical work. I had a very good academic upbringing, and was headed toward a pre-pharmacy program simply because I had gone to a drug store so many times as a kid to receive eye drops; it was a pleasant experience that left me with a wanting to work there. Consequently I thought I knew what I was going to do with my life. I went into a pre-pharmacy program for the first couple years, having received a scholarship from the Freeman Drug Company in River Falls, Wisconsin that helped pay for books.

Everything went well for I had acquired good study habits and an incentive to study. The first year was repetitive of high school. With regard to the pre-pharmacy program, something quite abruptly changed my career the second year. My advisor, while I was in the pre-professional program, was Dr. Kate Lineman a botany professor from UW-RF. I had been in a couple of her botany classes, which were prerequisites for pre-pharmacy and had learned that a lot of herbs and plants could be used for medicinal purposes. I knew her pretty well, and liked her and had received two A+s from her because I was able to memorize so well, like the long sequences of plant phyla. She always was impressed when she could write the letters across the board and I could repeat them for her though I was unable to see.

However in quantitative chemistry lab one day, Dr. Lineman approached me. She grabbed my shoulder and said, "Weberg, I gotta talk to you."

I followed her to her office. She had me sit and said, "Really, you have no business going into pharmacology because of your poor vision. You may have a tendency to perhaps hurt somebody or it may be unsafe for you. I think you probably better look for another major, something that does not have a chance to harm anybody. Maybe an area without a lab attached to it might be good."

It was quite a shock to me; because I had planned my whole life to go to pharmacy school at the University of Wisconsin and later, to work in a small town pharmacy, much like the one I had visited several times during my childhood. I was still visiting a pharmacy to put medication in my eyes. The decision was heart breaking. I remember crying and sulking about it. I went to Dr. Lineman a second and third time but she insisted that it was the best thing for me. I finally accepted it but to this day, every time I walk into a pharmacy I wish I were working there. I brooded about that for a while.

Fortunately, I had Mrs. Steiner at the country school, to go back to. She had indoctrinated us so well in all areas, whether it was English, history, science, math, or just life, that it was fairly easy for me to pick another area that didn't involve a laboratory. And after considerable thought, I decided to go into mathematics, simply because my uncle, Norris Weberg, was a genius at mathematics. He had been a farmer all his life but in his 50's, converted over to be an insurance agent for Mutual Trust Insurance Company. He had a fantastic mind for remembering numbers. I remember him dealing with clients at the table or at their house when we'd go visit him from time to time. He would be able to forecast for the client how much an annuity would cost 20 years out with regard to the amount of payment that the guy would have to be making each month for the first 20 years, and also 20 years before he may receive some kind of benefits. Oftentimes when they'd check the book and talked to the company, they found that Uncle Norris was right on. The book was off a couple cents, or whatever might be the deal. I enjoyed talking with him; he was very interesting with regard to knowing about algebra and mathematics, so I was pretty much inclined to go that direction.

My father was somewhat of the same nature, even though he didn't realize he was doing algebra. He was though, whenever he mixed the starter for the cheese in the morning at the early hours. He was using some form of algebra to determine how much of the starter he would put into the large vat of milk that would start to produce the cheese later in the day.

I switched over from the pre-pharmacy program to a major in math. Still, it broke my heart and it's kind of haunted me all my life, simply because every time I go into a pharmacy I remember my original desire. I didn't have the same equipment then that I have now to enable me to do the work because 45 years ago there were no Closed Curcuit TVs and talking computers.

So, I majored in mathematics and basically, had enough chemistry from pre-pharmacy to minor in it. I didn't know where I'd ever use it, because of the limitations that Dr. Lineman had mentioned to me. I didn't have any idea what I was going to do with a math degree either, other than going through college with straight A work and graduating with honors at UW-RF.

So therefore, I was tickled pink to have an opportunity to work at Control Data Corporation which, in the mid 60's, was a growing computer company. One of the kids I had played with as a child in Ellsworth, Wisconsin was Steve Guest. He had an older sister with bright red hair and she was a manager at Control Data. Steve took me to her house in River Falls, and I talked with her about having the desire to do some kind of programming or systems analyst work with Control Data. Two weeks later I received a call from her husband. He was a big honcho at Control Data; and he invited me in for an interview. Two days later I received an offer in the mail. I was elated and thrilled, to no end. Here I was, just a college graduate and I had gotten an offer from one of the major companies. It was Control Data, IBM, and Cray Research that were competitive at that time.

4. WORKING AND MARRIAGE

I went to work for Control Data the first part of June in 1965 and was assigned a position as Programmer Analyst to do programming for the Opcon Naval Project and discovered it was interesting. The U.S. Navy desired to locate ships and their cargo in both the Atlantic and Pacific Oceans. They needed a program written to actually do this type of analysis for the Navy, to discern whether that particular boat was a cargo or a military ship. We had various tests of the program that would analyze foreign ships, to determine whether they were domestic or enemy ships. It was fascinating to be part of writing this program. I wrote several sections of it and another colleague from the University of Wisconsin, Bill McCuen wrote the other part and we worked together on the Opcon system.

It was approximately a year later on a Tuesday that I was just finishing lunch when my vision went totally black on me. Bill and I told Dora Guest, who was in a nearby office. I said, "I have a problem here because I can't see anything."

I had been putting eye drops in. They took me to an eye doctor (ophthalmologist), to Minneapolis at the Minneapolis Eye Institute where Dr. Malcolm McCannell was the main glaucoma specialist. He was a friend of Dr. E. R. Jonas who knew me. Dr. Jonas had helped me with several things while I was growing up in Ellsworth. He had always been there to help out, in scouting and with health issues.

Jonas received a phone call from McCannell, and two days later I was having glaucoma surgery. The pressure in my eyes had zoomed up very high and that's why I lost my vision. The pressure was incredibly high and they did one of the first surgeries called a gonio puncture (making an opening in the top of the eye which lets out some vitreous humor). The problem with glaucoma is the vitreous humor does not flow out like it typically would in the normal eye.

I was admitted to a small hospital in Minneapolis called Eitel Hospital. It was strictly for eye patients. I had my head in sandbags for a number of days, packed in ice. A week later I was able to see a little out of the left eye. It was then that I started to recover.

Upon further examination it was found that the opening did not stay apart. Dr. McCannell had to redo the surgery in each eye; this time, sewing around the opening and leaving out a flap of skin in one end of each slit. That flap worked very much like the medical trashcans that they step on and the flap comes up. It was the same with this surgery, when the vitreous humor was ready to bubble out, the skin flap would stand up and the vitreous humor would flow over the eyeball and basically become the aqueous humor. When done, the flap would fall back down.

Each eye was done three times to get through the reduction of the high pressures between 45 and 60 millimeters of mercury on the surface of the eye. The normal pressure for a human eye is between 9 and 20 millimeters of mercury. This took several months, but I was still pretty much enthralled with the idea of getting a Master's degree and moving on in that direction academically because of my very good educational upbringing.

Dr. Jonas knew my situation of not being able to become a pharmacist and that I had a good mathematics background. I ended up with a year and a half of medical leave, and then terminated my employment with Control Data. From there I went to the University of Minnesota in the Department of Medical Statistics, where I was able to resume my career academically and study that particular area. Jonas had told me that it would combine my love for the pharmacy area with my desire and my ability to do mathematics and statistics. I worked there for a couple years and did all the course work; wrote a thesis for the department, and then went through preliminary exams and oral exams for the Masters degree. I was awarded the Master's degree in Biostatistics in August of 1968.

I came to this juncture of my life concerning my education. I was still located near the town of River Falls, Wisconsin, not exactly knowing what I was going to do with the degree I had earned. I had not received any further work in the field of medical statistics. I was at the Erickson Supermarket on a Saturday afternoon, shopping. Dr. Lillian Goff, from River Falls, approached me and asked me what I was doing at the present. I answered, "Well, I just received my Master's degree at the U of Minnesota, but I have not made any decision about what I am going to do with it."

She said, "I don't know if you'd be interested or not, but I have two assistant professor positions that are open in the Math Department for the fall term." It was late August and the fall term was starting in September. She said, "I think…just knowing you as a student, that you would do a very good job; plus, you now have a Master's degree, so you qualify for teaching there, with no problem."

I thanked her for the invitation and went home and thought about it over the weekend. The following Tuesday I called her up and said, "I think I'll give it a try, because it would make life easier. I'd not have to drive any distance to find work, like I was doing with Control Data."

I started in September of 1968 teaching mathematics. There were a couple trigonometry courses and an algebra course the first term and they worked well. I had no idea that I was ever going to do any teaching. I had thought that I was headed strictly into industry, or something along the research or pharmacy line but I discovered that I like teaching. I had a nice schedule, 12 hours a week in the classroom and a lot of preparation that first year (getting lectures ready and preparing exams). I enjoyed working with the students, not only in the classroom, but when they needed help and came in with questions; it seemed natural. The best part of teaching at the University was that I didn't have to drive anyplace. I could just walk back and forth from my home to the office.

I taught mathematics for a year and at the end of the spring term I was hired as a permanent professor. I was a 24 years old with a lot of ambition.

In November of 1968 I married Jean Reister after 3 years of dating. Jean was a registered nurse with a 4-year college education and a bachelor's degree. We had a good marriage, living in a smaller town of River Falls with 20,000 people, including all the students. We had a very close and intimate relationship for many years.

Two children blessed are lives. Mark was born in 1971 and we adopted Stephanie in 1976. The marriage ended 21 years later, due to my gambling addiction. It ended after I had been in recovery from gambling for 8 years. Jean still felt the emotional pain caused by the gambling. Today, I'm thankful for the marriage Jean and I had and I ask God's blessing upon her.

It was the summertime of 1969 and all the academic people were there nine months and off for three. I didn't want to sit around for three months, so I made application to Control Data again, to IBM at Rochester, Minnesota and Sperry Univac in St. Paul, Minnesota.

I received offers to all three places. I had decided that I had been at Control Data for a long enough period of time and thought I'd try one of the other two. When we drove to Rochester it was an extremely long drive, and I knew I didn't have a way of getting back and forth, other than driving myself. Again, vision limited me.

I found people who lived in Prescott, Wisconsin and worked at Sperry Univac, so I made an arrangement with some of them to carpool. I began my career in the Education Department of the Defense Systems Division during the summertime. And it happened that during the school year as well, for a couple days during the week and vacations that I was able to work there. It was a nice consulting position, one in which I could accomplish a lot of things in the education area with regard to the writing of textbooks and teaching small seminars.

Dr. Goff, the same lady who hired me, thought that this was a good thing because of all the experience I was getting with the Navy applications; it would be advantageous for students to hear that. So she arranged my schedule in order to enable me to teach Monday, Wednesday, Friday, and go to Sperry Univac on Tuesday and Thursday. It was good for me, a change from the classroom at the college to working in industry with the people that were former Navy folks. It is a pleasant memory. In fact, I continued that consulting position from 1969 to 1979, and it was an especially fine time in my life that I had a combination of the academic and the business world.

5. DRINKING AND GAMBLING

I made some good friends at Sperry. It was during that time as a young man, because of the eye problems, that I developed serious inferiority complexes. I felt worthless next to other people, that I wasn't as good as them. These thoughts roamed in my head.

I went to drinking, on weekends mainly. I never did any during the week, because it was firmly indoctrinated in me to do the best job I could in whatever I did. I would reward myself on the weekends with too much to drink. I drank in the college town and at Sperry as well, as there were a lot of drinker-type people there. They were Navy people who would go out for lunch and it'd be three hours before we got back. The folks I rode with from Prescott were no exceptions to that. Sometimes we'd get home at 7:00 or 8:00 in the evening, rather than 4:00 and 5:00 in the afternoon, because of going to the valley to drink beer after the workday was over. It was at that point I ran into a guy I used to drink with. Al was his name, and he approached me one day and asked if I'd ever done any gambling.

"Not really," I said. "I played a little penny ante poker when I was in college." (I would tell people the next day I'd played poker all night; it was sort of a macho trip.) And that is how my gambling career started. It seemed to fit in well with my mathematics background and I began by betting with Al on football games.

Al had been a drinking buddy for a couple years and asked me about the gambling thing. I said, "I don't know anything about it."

He said, "Well, I'll tell you what to do." What we do, he explained, is use one of the services that he was working with. That service picked

22

games and was giving him those picks, like 3 college and 3 professional games. He would obtain the picks on a Thursday evening, and then contact 1 or 2 bookies (people who'd take the bets). He would get what's called "the line on a game."

He told me all about this over our drinking coffee one day, and asked me if I would be interested in trying.

I said, "What does it cost to do that?"

And he said "Well it's like a minimum of a $50 bet, if you want to do it."

I had never done any betting before, but he said he'd been winning on it quite a bit so it intrigued me and I ended up putting $100 on each of the six games for our first weekend in the fall of 1969.

Later Friday evening, he called me back over in Wisconsin. He said, "This is what you have, it's the same thing I have. We have this team, plus so many points. This team, minus so many points, and so forth."

There were three colleges and three pro. I didn't think much more about it but the following Monday morning when I rode in with the carpool, and walked into the Sperry Univac office, I glanced up at the clock. It was a couple minutes after 8:00 in the morning, and I saw Al come walking down the hallway.

I said, "How did we do?" and I thought, *is this gambling, or what?*

And he said, "We won all six!"

It was hard for me to fathom, because that was like $600 that Monday morning. And, at that time, I was doing this consulting thing for like $50 a day, or making $250 a week driving back and forth and going through the hassle of an eight-hour day. So it seemed really simple. I didn't know it, but it was a psychological hook placed inside my head at that point. I wanted to do it next weekend again! I did not want to let it go by. The following week we were again six for six. I said, "I can't believe it."

It's like $1,200 that's very easy to pick up. And the third weekend it was five out of six. That first year, in using the service, I ended up $25,000 to $30,000 ahead. I could not believe it; it was so simple to do. The football season ended with a strong desire to look forward to the next season. I used the same system the second year and was again successful; and I made a good amount of money. Having an analyst's mind, I was ready to quit the 'rink-a-dink' work and move to Las Vegas.

I wanted my livelihood to be gambling. I needed to move someplace where I could be in the game all the time. It wasn't enough to merely lay wagers on Friday and Saturday. It had become necessary for me to gamble full time.

Thus, the need for gambling got a hold of me and would not let go. From 1969 to 1982, a 13 year span of gambling controlled me. At the same time I was working at Sperry Univac and teaching at the University. The bets were no longer $100, but $200, then $300, and finally $500 per game. The fourth year we had a break-even time and figured it would go back up the following year. Well, the fifth year it did not go back up, but went down a fair amount. Al and I both had to start averaging out income because our bets were higher. The two of us were betting together and we completely trusted each other.

The gambling continued on and I was having eye problems again and had to have more surgeries. In 1977 I was still teaching at the University. I would teach algebra and calculus for the 12 hour a week that I was required to. While teaching I was helping students and I enjoyed that.

6. FAMILY

I maintained a family at the time. Jean, my wife, and I had a son that we named Mark. I thought life was exciting. Bringing up a child, being a part of the home and still, always being involved with the betting in a secretive way was a challenge I enjoyed. I gambled and other people did not know about it, until problems in the household took over and I discovered it was not a secret anymore.

My son was born in 1971. He had brilliant red hair like his mom. He was a cute little boy with regard to many different things growing up. It was nice to have a young man in the family. It wasn't too long after he was born that my brother, Ron said, "Hey Lyn, you better look at his eyes. They look just like yours when you were small."

Sure enough, Mark ended up having glaucoma and when he was about six months old we took him to the ophthalmologist, Dr. Malcolm McCannell, and his colleague, Brooks Poley. Mark was approximately a year old when he had eye surgery to eliminate the problem of the glaucoma.

Mark was a captivating child, with his red hair and freckles. A lot of the colleagues at the University, especially Dr. Lila Olson, would tell me from time to time that he should be in commercials. It wasn't long after that, that I signed him up for doing commercials with a couple different companies, and he was auditioned. One of the auditions was with the Play Mobile Toy Company, and that one came through for Mark. He was in a national magazine showing their toys, and with his freckled face and red hair it made a charming picture.

I also remember another audition where we got a call from Campbell's Soup Company. They needed a kid with red hair to audition their tomato soup. I took Mark to Minneapolis on a Friday afternoon. Going into the hotel room was a startling experience, to see about 40 red haired and freckled children. The whole room was filled with red hair and freckles! Campbell Soup people tried out each kid with a smile; it turned out that Mark didn't get it.

However, McDonald's Corporation called him the very next day. We went to an audition for McDonald's; he and a little girl sat at a table in a restaurant. They were both sipping malts and eyeing each other with a big McDonald's sign on the other side of the table.

Another time we flew to Chicago. It was a cereal commercial which he did not get selected for, but he thought the trip was fun. It was interesting, and he was happy to have those opportunities.

Because of the way Mark's eyes were when he was born, the doctors suggested we adopt if we wanted another child. Mark was five and we started the process of adopting another child. We wanted a little girl. Mark and Jean both had red hair. The social worker asked me, "Do you want the child to have red hair like your son and wife?"

I said, "Not really. Red hair is nice, but I don't want to be overwhelmed by it."

"Well, we can arrange it," she said, "So the child would fit in."

Lutheran Social Services interviewed us extensively. We definitely wanted to have a baby girl. They were responsible for finding us a child. It was in 1976 that we acquired a new member to our family, our little girl.

We were notified they had a daughter for us. For five hours we drove across Wisconsin to Appleton, in a 1972 Pontiac, Grand Prix. Mark was excited. He was one happy little five-year-old boy because he was going to get his new sister.

In Appleton we stopped in front of an old, red house that sat on a relatively large size pond of water. There was a sign above the doorway: *Lutheran Social Services*. We walked in and identified ourselves to the receptionist. She said, "Well, if you'd wait a couple minutes, I'll make the arrangements for you to see your baby."

We waited 15 minutes. The lady came out and said, "You now can come in and see this little baby girl, and decide if you want her or not."

I told her, "Lady, I've come across the State of Wisconsin to pick up my daughter today. There's no question about whether I want her or not. We're picking up our baby and Mark's sister right now."

So, we walked in the room and admired our new little girl. She was 17 inches long and weighed about nine pounds. She was a cute little girl, and it was immediate love for each of us. We were overjoyed to have the opportunity to take her home with us. On the way home Mark was jumping up and down and bouncing around with enthusiasm in the back seat; he really did have a baby sister now!

We named her Stephanie and she was a little girl that fit very well in our family. When she grew a little older she didn't have red hair like the other two members, and she didn't have hair like mine, which is kind of blondish, but she had brunette hair with red highlights, and it fit our family especially well. Growing up, she worked out very nicely. We had a little boy and a little girl in our family, and my wife and me. It was a happy family in those days.

7. MEDICAL PROBLEMS

It was in the late '70's. The things Mrs. Steiner had taught me continued to be a part of me. Even after having a Master's degree and teaching in Wisconsin, I found myself going back to graduate school to work on my PhD. It was because Mrs. Steiner, the country schoolteacher, had always instilled in me that you should not quit until you actually finish the job, and to me this meant getting my highest education degree. It was that process, along with raising a family, teaching, consulting at Sperry Univac, and doing some gambling on the side that I found myself extremely busy.

It was during this time that additional medical problems arose, especially in the area of kidney function. I had not realized that when you're born with congenital anomalies, they come in pairs, or sometimes triplets. The glaucoma had been the obvious one but now, all of a sudden, I was faced with the fact that my kidney function was dropping below 10% (it was not attributed to excess drinking). I knew because I'd asked several doctors about it. They said, "No, it is a congenital anomaly and it was inevitable that your kidney function was going to reduce."

So, in late '76, early '77, I had to go on dialysis, which complicated things. I had to take a medical leave of absence from the University of Wisconsin. Sperry was always good to me because they would allow me to take work with me to do while I was away. I started to go to Rochester, Minnesota, for dialysis because my nephrologist was there. Being relatively young I was placed on a transplant list because my health was overall quite good. I was on the list for almost a year when

28

my younger brother, Ron, decided that he would donate one of his kidneys to me.

Both of my kidneys, the spleen and appendix had been surgically removed from my body. It was August 4, 1977. The transplant surgeon, Sterioff, said, "I'm going to do this today and you won't want to have anybody around you for about three days because you'll feel so terrible, so miserable." Then he added, "We'll give you a private room and keep the door closed except for lunch and stuff like that."

He was absolutely right because the Senior Pastor from our church, Jewel Burnt (PhD), visited me on the second day and I pretty much told him off on short order, that I didn't want to talk to him, and sent him away. It was an extremely hard time; I had a lot of pain in my back, my abdominal area and everywhere else. I apologized later to Pastor Burnt.

On September 9, 1977, Ron donated one of his kidneys, and that was sure a memorable day. My brother had been checked out to be a donor. I was immensely thankful to him, not only that day, but for the rest of my life. I thanked him for stepping forward and giving a part of his body to help me in my situation. At this time I ask God to bless you, Ron, to help you in every way, from this point on. Dear brother, I'll always be filled with gratitude for what you did for me.

I went to surgery, consecutively with my brother. Before sleep, I remember Dr. Sterioff coming to my room. He had my brother's kidney in his hands, and he said, "Lyn, this is a gift of life from your brother to you, and I'm now going to put it into your body and hook it up so you'll be able to live normally again."

I was groggy, but clearly remember seeing that, and was very impressed by actually setting eyes on the kidney, and knowing where it was going in my body.

I received that transplant on September 9, 1977 and started to live with my brother's kidney. I talked with him the next day and he showed me the big "S" cut into his side where they had removed his right kidney. Fortunately, God gives us much more kidney function than we really need, so we are able to live in good health with one kidney. Ron has been fine ever since with one; and at that point in time, I had the other one inside my body. It allowed me not to have to go to dialysis.

I spent time recovering at the kidney transplant area on the fifth floor of Rochester Methodist Hospital in Rochester, Minnesota. It was brought to my attention, after four months recovery that I should enroll in what they call the 'ADD Unit' (Alcohol Drug and Dependency Unit), in order to learn to live without drinking. It was located on the Ninth Floor of the same building.

I took the elevator to the fifth floor and there learned the 12 steps of AA (Alcoholic Anonymous), and started to recover from alcoholism. I spent 30 days in the program, learning how to live without dependence. In each of the steps I made decisions, and amends and inventories. It was an incredible program. In the end I had gone through the steps, and 30 days clean with no drinking.

In Step 1 I admitted I was powerless over alcohol (and gambling) and that living had become unmanageable. I wanted to rebuild my life without the two addictions. The fourth step was inventory. I spent a week and a half listing in a notebook all the things I had done wrong. Then I made an appointment with a pastor at the hospital to do the Fifth Step. I admitted to God and another person the exact nature of my wrongs (I went and dumped the dump truck full of all the stuff I'd done). I was ready to start over again. It took about six hours to accomplish the Fifth Step. The minister was willing to sit and listen, interrupting now and then with his opinions or questions. Toward the end he said "Now I want you to list the positives from your teaching and consulting and affirmative things that you've done in your life. Let's talk about those for a while, as well."

So, I made a list of those and talked to him about them. He said, "This is what you'll build your new life on. The fact that you've had all this other stuff happen with medical and drinking and gambling – now, you have a new opportunity to live without it."

Again the Christian upbringing that I had at home, when my mom used to read to me and show me pictures in the Bible, all pretty much fell in line with the recovery program. I knew I wanted to have a good life.

So I left the ADD Unit a month later with no drinking and no gambling in my life, and that lasted for almost a year. I stayed around Rochester in recovery for several months. It was toward the end of four months when suddenly the transplanted kidney did not work anymore. I was back in the hospital with all kinds of biopsies and tests, and everything else that they could possibly do to try and get it going again because it had been functioning well for almost half of a year. The creatinine was running around 1.4, 1.5 where it should be for a transplanted person.

During this time I had an excessive amount of Salumetrol and Lasix intravenously and that took away the high frequencies of my hearing as well. For a person who does not see well, I depended heavily on hearing for many years and now that was somewhat damaged as well. From that point on, I had to have hearing aids in order to converse with those around me.

The kidney refused to work anymore, so it was removed. That was a sad, sad day for my brother, when they took his kidney out of me and put it in a jar. It is now in the museum at the Mayo Clinic, as an example of a transplanted kidney. I was without any kidneys again.

One morning while still in the hospital, a big, old tough Army nurse informed me, "Weberg, you're going to dialysis today."

She rolled me out of bed. I hadn't had dialysis for six months so it was quite a shock to visit the dialysis unit and get plugged in for revamping and cleaning out the body again. When I started back on dialysis, it was heartbreaking for my brother. He was down in the dumps about it and I had to talk to him several times, explaining how he'd given me a good six months with no dialysis and just how thankful I was to him. I still appreciated what he did. I was positive he had done the best he could. So I found myself back on dialysis and back on the transplant list.

One time I took my family on vacation to Disney World in Orlando, Florida. The children enjoyed the rides. We were having dinner in the evening. Everything was going fine – in fact, it was going so well that I said, "Well, I might as well add to it by having a drink and gambling again."

That was a restart of what I had done before, and it wasn't too much longer after that, that I was back on dialysis. It was not ever attributed to that, but it was so disappointing and so disheartening! To be with my wife Jean and my children, Mark and Stephanie one day, and now here I was back on dialysis, in order to maintain life. I agonized about it for quite a while but then remembered my mother's quotes from the

Bible of "The joy of the Lord is our strength!" and "God gives us no more than what we can handle" and "Come unto me all you who are heavy laden, and I shall give you rest."

Mother and Dad would drive from Ellsworth, WI to Rochester, MN to spend time with me. I am still thankful for their visits in Rochester. I was so blessed by having such great parents! They were surely picked out for me by God!

During the second time on dialysis I figured that's where I was going to end up, because at Mayo Clinic there's row after row of people on the machines that have been there for 10, 15 or 20 years. For such a long time they ran their life around coming to dialysis three times a week. So I was back in the same situation again. I didn't know what I was to do because I couldn't see to read with the poor vision, and I couldn't sit and listen to tapes. Finally, my father said, "Maybe you should start some kind of business here. Maybe we can do that."

He knew I liked to talk and sell. So I ended up starting a stock brokerage business while on dialysis (that's a story in itself). He built me a tabletop for the dialysis unit. I went through training for getting my licenses for both Minnesota and Wisconsin. My academic background made that fairly easy to do. I started selling stock while on dialysis. Almost with a PhD, I was on the dialysis machine selling stock. At that time, there was a new company out of Denver, called Denver Electronics Corporation, Denel Corp, by acronym, which had an advanced computer processor over Cray Research, and I knew the difference. Cray Research had done very well and was like a $20, $30 stock; Denel Corp was like a $2 or $3 stock. I talked to people about buying Denel Corp., and they bought thousands of shares. Many doctors at Mayo Clinic were some of my first clients. They bought thousands of shares at $2 and $3 for Denel Corp. And it wasn't much longer, six months, seven months, that the stock was like $10, $12, $13 a share and then ultimately, went up to $25 to $30. A lot of those same people sold the stock and made a large amount of money. Then they asked me, "What should I buy next?" I sold them International Dairy Queen at $6, and that too did really well.

The gambling was persisting. If there was any point in my life where the gambling was somewhat beneficial (I don't like to say this too loudly, but, to give hope when on dialysis, because it's a hopeless situation), it was then. I would go every other day to get pumped out for six or eight hours, head home and sleep, feel pretty good the next half a day, and then go back on the machine again; it was a wild life. I was able to look at the latest line in the newspaper and make a decision about whatever I was going to bet on. I called the bookies and felt it was an enlightening thing because it gave me something to look forward to. It kept me busy.

Mayo Clinic was especially good at arranging vacations for their dialysis patients. I made a vacation request to go to Las Vegas while on dialysis. My wife had gone to Las Vegas a few times with me before and we enjoyed the shows, and I had a chance to gamble there.

In early 1978, I needed to dialyze at the Sunray Hospital, just off the strip. I walked in to get on the dialysis machine. A large heavyset nurse said, "Well, we do not have one here."

They didn't even know what a dialysis machine was! Finally, another person said, "Yeah, we have one that's in this other room over here; it's under the bed."

So they got the dialysis machine out. I'd been used to pretty sophisticate equipment at the Mayo Clinic. They brought out this old washtub-looking thing that had rubber hoses with needles at the end. I made an excuse and left. I didn't really want to have it done there so I called Mayo Clinic and said, "You've got to give me another recommendation because they don't even know what they're doing across the street here."

I was sent to another hospital where they had somewhat more similar equipment to what Mayo Clinic had.

I was staying at Caesar's Palace when I got a call on April 1st, 1978, from Dr. Sylvester Sterioff, the transplant surgeon at Mayo Clinic. That evening, I'd been gambling most of the day and had a pretty good winning streak going. I went to bed at 2:00 or 3:00 in the morning when the call came in. Jean said I should answer the phone; I did, and it was Dr. Sterioff. He said, "Come back as soon as you can because I have another kidney coming in from Cincinnati."

I was excited to hear such news.

"A young man has been shot and his kidney is an exact match to what you need." He added, "Even a better match than your brother."

The next day we left at 9:00 a.m., boarded the plane, and flew back to Minneapolis. Dale and Lila Birkel, friends of ours, came to the airport to pick us up and we all headed down Highway 52 toward Rochester, Minnesota. I remember that day well, because there was a new 17 inches of wet, fresh snow that made it more or less like sliding down the road to Rochester, rather than driving sensibly. We glided into the hospital parking lot sometime during the late afternoon.

I checked in, and from 10 p.m. to 3a.m. had dialysis, hopefully for the last time. Then I went in to have a transplant once again, and they placed the cadaver kidney on the opposite side from where my brother's kidney had been. I felt very blessed to have another opportunity, with a second transplant. I was off the dialysis machine again, and walking around with a working kidney inside me. I'm very thankful to this day. Now it's been more than a quarter of a century and I'm still free of dialysis! I really am thankful–thankful to that cadaver and thankful to my brother for his efforts.

The stock brokerage work was going better than I had expected. We moved back to River Falls. I took a leave of absence from the University and continued to sell stock. Denel Corp., by that time, had gone up to $15.00, $18.00, $20.00 a share. All the doctors at Mayo Clinic said, "Well, should we sell it?" "What should we do?" And I told them, "I think it's got a little bit more." We waited until it was in the low 30's; then they sold it. And of course, their next question for me was, "What do you have next?"

As a result, I put a lot of people on to International Dairy Queen and a couple others (2 of the 3 did well). I found it really interesting. Lillian Goff, a widow lady, had never invested in anything and I talked her into buying 2,000 shares of Dairy Queen at $6.00 a share. She did, but didn't watch it. She'd just call me every once in a while and ask how it was doing. Three to eight months would go by, and I'd hear from her again. Finally down the road, she was able to sell that for $30-some-dollars a share; she was elated. She said, "I just didn't think that anything would do that well!" It was a treat for me to be able to show her how to do it.

The brokerage business was doing nicely. I ran into a senior broker named Silverman and he told me I could use something called "A Care of Address" routine to sell stock out of state, since Wisconsin was one of the toughest states. I did some of that with a company called Ionic Controls, and sold to everyone in my book.

After a year in the business I received a call from the State Securities Department saying they wanted to come and review my books. They asked, "What is this that you have written in the book?"

I didn't think there was anything wrong with it. I said, "Well, that's a "care of address" for the stock Ionic Controls, which isn't registered in Wisconsin but is in Minnesota. If people in Wisconsin want to buy it, I have them go through a friend or relative in Minnesota."

And the man from the state, Terry Nelson, said, "That's not legal. We have to indict you, more or less for doing something grossly wrong."

I had a couple hundred of those in my book. So that started the legal problems with the brokerage business. I had to pay a fine and be on probation for a period of time.

During this time I continued to gamble. The brokerage business was such that I could sell stocks during the daytime and gamble at night. It was really quite a mess, quite a maze, and my bets had gone to $1,000, $2,000 a bet, rather than being low like they were before. So definitely, the addiction of gambling was part of my life and it continued on right through that brokerage scenario.

Back in business, I went to a couple different brokerage houses over in Minnesota and continued to sell stock. Now having an office at Lakeland, Minnesota, I sold stock there. When I was shut down in River Falls it caused legal problems. I remember having a one year probation and a fine of a couple thousand dollars.

At the same time, the gambling bets were getting bigger and bigger. It was hard for me to delineate which was which sometimes. Sell stock during the daytime, gamble at night, back and forth. I'd been with two brokerage companies while in Wisconsin and, when this happened; a third brokerage company approached me. They knew I was a good salesman and asked me to join their firm in Minnesota. That company was called Alstead, Strangis & Dempsey. They were located in Minnetonka, Minnesota, a western suburb of Minneapolis.

I went for an interview with Jerry Alstead, and he said he wanted me to come onboard because he knew I'd done good work for the other two companies. I told him of the limitation with my vision. I said, "I cannot drive over here every day. You'll have to think about setting up a branch office for me someplace, so I can get there a little quicker and a little easier."

He asked me where I lived and I told him. I told him of the recent problem in Wisconsin. I said I needed to locate in Minnesota someplace. He set me up in a little town called Afton, Minnesota, located close to the St Croix River. He set me up in an office there because I had a principal's license; therefore, I could run the office the way I had been running it before. I had a secretary at the time named Joan. She lived in River Falls, the same town I lived in, and she drove me every day over there and back because of my inability to drive. I was working there, selling stocks that Alstead wanted me to sell, being careful not to do the "care of address" thing anymore.

I was able to do a large job for Alstead, Strangis. In fact, when they had their first Christmas party, they sent someone over to get me because I'd been the second highest producer in the company. It was usually no problem for me to sell, along with being a good college professor, I was a good salesman. The only guy ahead of me in sales was the middle guy in the company, John Strangis, and he was a big, burly man. I told him at the Christmas party, "Next year, John, I'm gonna beat you out for this position."

This kind of arrogance went along with being in the stock brokerage business. It didn't stop there, but continued on. They would give certain incentives through the company; for instance, if you could sell five groups of Energy Shed stock at $5,000 a group, they would give you a free trip to Acapulco. I did that within a week or ten day period. I sold to five different people $5,000 amounts, which is like 5,000 shares of Energy Shed at a time; and then went on a trip to Acapulco for 10 days because of it.

They worked a lot with new issues, whatever their new issues were. I would be able to sell those to the people, hoping to get a good start when they began to trade. And it was late 1979, early 1980. I was sitting in the office one day and out of my window I saw a man with an old, but good looking car drive up. It was an old car but was well polished, and it looked like a neat car. He got out of his vehicle, and Joan told me that someone was here to talk about investments.

So she brought him in and he introduced himself as Bill C. He had on bright yellow pants with a yellow and red polo shirt. His outfit was worth remembering. I was sitting there with a three piece suit on, like a stock-broker-image. He asked if he could shut the door. And then told me he had gotten a call from a family member with regard to my gambling. He had come to try and give me some insight to what was called "Gamblers Anonymous."

The man told me his story about how he'd been a gambler and how he'd found recovery in Gamblers Anonymous. He read to me out of this little yellow book, a combo book, as he called it, about the steps of recovery. I was fairly familiar with those because of the AA program. He spoke about several other things in the book and invited me to come to a GA meeting some night soon. He said, "I'd be willing to drive over and pick you up. I know that you can't see well enough to make it on your own."

A couple nights later I thought I better check it out. I called him, and he drove over and took me to the first meeting of Gamblers Anonymous. I sent Joanie home at the regular time and told her I'd see her the next day. The meeting was at a church in St. Paul, Minnesota, on a Wednesday evening. I had to answer 20 questions about whether I had a gambling problem or not. I think I answered 18 yes and two no, and they all told me I was in the right place to get help.

They proceeded to read out of the combo book, then took a break, and had a therapy session after that. It seemed to me when anybody spoke that evening; it fit me pretty well I had experienced some phase of what they said about their gambling. It came my turn and I talked about my situation, of how I had encountered legal problems and marital problems because of the gambling.

Afterwards, Bill drove me to River Falls back to my home. He was happy to do it. He said, "Can I be your temporary sponsor?"

I answered him, "Sure, you can."

And he said, "Well, that means you can call me day or night if you feel like gambling, I don't want you to gamble any more. But I can't make that decision; you have to make it. Here's a couple numbers."

I don't believe he had a cell phone at that time, but he reassured me, "Call me, day or night, if you have an urge to gamble. I'll talk to you on the phone, or come and pick you up, or whatever we need to do."

So, I thanked him very much. He asked, "Well, can I come and pick you up on the weekend for another meeting?"

And I said, "Yeah, that'd be all right."

I attended another meeting with Bill, and started to go pretty regularly on Wednesday evenings to the St. Paul meeting. He told my wife about a sister program called Gam-Anon that would help her handle my gambling and recovery. It wasn't too long after that Jean started to drive me in on a Wednesday evening so Bill did not have to come after me. I'd go to the GA meeting and she would attend the Gam-Anon meeting; that worked out well. Attending that program, I discovered it did help me stop gambling.

The brokerage business was still doing proficiently well. In June of 1982 (I stopped drinking 3, 4 months earlier that year) I felt much better. I was at the office. Joan picked up the paper she'd brought from home. She said, "Look at the headlines here. It says, 'Alstead, Strangis & Dempsey, huge legal problems.'"

I said, "Oh, my God."

All of their stocks had gone in the tank because someone had done some incorrect things there, and all the stocks I had sold from that company went down drastically; therefore, people lost a lot of money. There were more legal problems because of it.

While I had been attending Gamblers Anonymous, I had continued in the stock brokerage business. With all this going on, my wife didn't want to have anything else to do with me. I had hurt a lot of people, not only in Wisconsin but also in Minnesota. I stayed in a lake home up north. I had been off the gambling for quite a while, but the pressures of everything in my life at that time caused me to go back to gambling once more. The lake home was located at Lake Magnor, Wisconsin. After living there for a while, I called the University. I had been away 3 years on a medical leave of absence. In the late summer I called them and spoke with the Associate Dean of the College, a man by the name of Dr. Dick DeLaura (PhD). I knew him fairly well, and told him what my situation was, and that I'd like to have another chance at the University.

He said, "Well, you've always done good work here. Let me talk to the Chairman of the Math Department and see what we can do to arrange for you to come back here for the fall term."

A few days later he called me back and said I could start in September. I was to attend the faculty meeting as I'd done before; they would have a full load for me to teach in the fall term.

I was staying at the lake home and felt fed up with the gambling, the shifting around of monies, and all the problems it caused. I made a decision to give Gamblers Anonymous another try, and called them. I asked where the next meeting was, and they said it was at St. Mary's Hospital in Minneapolis. It was fairly early that Sunday afternoon, so I caught a ride down to the freeway and hitchhiked into Minneapolis. Things were much safer in the area than they are now.

At St. Mary's Hospital (the meeting had just started), I was told I'd better clean up my act totally and get into the Gamblers Anonymous program again. I attended the GA meeting that evening. There were approximately 25 people in the room. I sat and listened, and answered the questions again, 19 out of 20 yes's in this case. I made a firm decision that I didn't want to gamble any more. And like Jim C. said, "You just indicate when you get up tomorrow morning that you choose not to gamble for the day. You choose not to, and choose not to, and choose not to all day long whenever you are tempted."

I had about six bookies at the time, so I had to tell them that I didn't want to gamble any more, and that I was choosing not to. I went through all this stuff, and had a lot of extra legal problems caused by the Alstead, Strangis experience; now I'd had two bad episodes of legal problems. I thought to myself, *well, my future is really in the academic area anyway!* So I went back to teaching.

I got slapped on the hand royally with another fine and another probation period. This time I had a probation officer who, for five years, worked with me while I was teaching at the University. It was not a real pleasant time because of the small-town atmosphere, the attention from the paper, and the fact that I had made several errors while getting back into gambling. But, I'm thankful to this day that the University of Wisconsin allowed me to teach the fall term there. I started to get my head on right, to live with the GA program, go to meetings every week (sometimes twice a week) and get back with my teaching. I did everything I needed to do with regard to the law. October 19, 1982 is my clean date of both gambling and drinking. From that date to this, I have been free of both addictions. I live on, with the absence of both gambling and drinking.

8. THE SPONSOR

Stafford, my sponsor in GA, helped me a great deal. He involved me in a number of things in my early recovery that were influential in my healing. We got a call one night; my wife and I were asked to go with them to the Twin Cities, to Eau Claire, Wisconsin. They were to speak on a panel against having a horseracing track in that town. They'd gotten a call from the Chamber of Commerce in Eau Claire to represent their side of the issue. Stafford wanted my wife and me to go along. He wanted just the four of us to participate. So, we did.

They picked us up in the late afternoon and we drove to Eau Claire, a relatively small town of 65,000 people. We were going to essentially give points against having a horseracing track there. We were asked many questions about what gambling does to a community. They asked, "What are the bad points of gambling, especially for the elderly and the poor?"

It was good for me to voice the answers. I told them, "This will wear away the fiber of the community; it'll get lower and lower, and you'll have people coming in the community that are not so desirable."

It was a good opportunity and we all talked and gave our opinions. When I left, I felt it was beneficial; giving the fathers of the community something to think about in regards to what happens when there's legalized gambling in their community.

Another time Stafford answered a call from people in Minneapolis. They wanted us to talk on a radio program, to answer questions about gambling. Is it bad? What's going on with gambling? How can I avoid it? He called me and said, "Lyn, I want you to come over for this broadcast and help me answer some questions."

So, we met at 5:30 or 6:30. It was a program where the radio announcer had an open mike for people to call in with questions about gambling, how bad it would be, or what the difference between a novice and a compulsive gambler was, and so forth. We spent time answering the questions.

One of the questions to me was. "What's the difference between gambling once every month, or three times a month, or every day?"

"There are different levels to gambling," I said. "You can be a trivial gambler, maybe betting once or twice in your life for what is usually a very small risk. Or you might be a social gambler that likes to go to places for the low-price dinner and show, and then plays a few hands of Black Jack or something. Then you go home and don't think any more about it for maybe a year. It just was kind of an entertainment evening. And there's, yet, another group that will go set a limit at what they can lose, whether it's $100.00 or $50.00 or $10.00. And, once that's done, they pick up and leave, whether they win, lose or whatever. For these people, it stays quite vividly in their minds. They find themselves returning the next time with a higher limit, and the same thing happens over and over again until they've got to come more frequently."

I went on to explain that usually the compulsive gambler is one who has had, sometime in the early gambling experience, a relatively large win. It made things look easy to that person and a psychological "hook" gets set in his mind.

I think back about the first time I bet. It was on 6 different football games, $100.00 each, and when I came back into work on Monday morning, Al said, "Hey, we won all six."

It was like $600.00 was over two weeks of salary at that time. And I was psychologically "hooked", especially when the next weekend it was 6 out of 6 again. The third weekend was 5 out of 6, and it was almost like I could do no wrong. It was so easy, fun, and macho! The 'big shot' attitude or psyche seemed so important and simply terrific! Yes, the psychological "hook" was set and I began gambling football games from that point on.

There was another time when Stafford contacted me and we went to a TV studio. They didn't show our faces because we were in the TV area for Minneapolis, St. Paul, and western Wisconsin, where I was from. All they actually showed was shadows where we sat. We answered questions from a panel on the things that were done in the Gamblers Anonymous program.

Again, there were all kinds of questions. "How can I tell if I'm a compulsive gambler?" "Where are the meetings for Gamblers Anonymous so I can check this out?" "Do you think I have a problem?" I responded by giving examples.

All of this was good for my recovery. It helped me to fortify the fact that, hey, I don't want to gamble anymore! Enough of my life had been spent in this destruction from 1969 to 1982. And I thank Stafford to this day for involving me in so many things, to actually being a part of what he wanted to accomplish. He didn't need to do that but knew I was in early recovery, and that it would strengthen me.

I also remember a lot of things about my sponsor, how once a year he would throw a big party at his house for GA people from all the meetings in Minneapolis, St. Paul, western Wisconsin and Iowa. Everybody would come to his house on a Saturday morning; he had a big swimming pool in the backyard. Everyone swam, and we had a fantastic day eating a lot of good food and having things to drink. If a person wanted to drink alcohol, he could, but there wasn't very much of that, mostly soda pop. Stafford would have a band in the evening.

The whole day was refreshing, and demonstrated to me the sincerity of my sponsor about wanting to give back to his family. They were there, his wife, children, and their children's children. He was a grandfather who played with his grandkids all that day; it was just a wonderful event. Every year we looked forward to it. I went 5 or 6 times and felt benefited by being part of his life those weekends.

Later on when I was doing my PhD. course work and being unable to see to drive, Stafford would be in touch with me and say, "Well, come over and stay at my house tonight, or for a couple nights until the weekend, and then you can head back home," or something of that nature.

He was an extraordinarily giving individual and I learned from that to be a giving individual as well or at least I think I'm doing that in my life.

9. MY CONVERSION - OCTOBER 19, 1982:

A PLUMBER BRINGS JESUS TO A PROFESSOR!

On October 19, 1982 (more than 25 years ago), a plumber named Bob Robertson was called to the lake home in northern Wisconsin, of Professor Lyndon C. Weberg, for a small plumbing job. When completed with his task, he asked the professor, "What're all these gambling forms scattered about on the kitchen table?"

I explained that I was close to ending my gambling addiction, but not quite yet. Bob, the plumber, sat down at the kitchen table and gave me his testimony about Jesus Christ. He explained, "For many years I'd been a drunken bum on skid row in St. Paul, Minnesota. I sure didn't feel good about myself. I knew my life was about over."

Bob the plumber looked me in the eye across the table and went on to say, "One cold night on skid row, while we were huddling together to keep warm, a street preacher came along and witnessed about Jesus. My associates and I listened to him. After some reluctance, I decided to accept Jesus. I was taken to a shelter for warmth and a bed for the night. And during the following days, the street preacher prayed with me and took me to church."

That was when things started to change for the better in Bob's life. That day the plumber willingly took 4 hours out of his day to give me his testimony, and how everything had gotten much better with no booze.

He ended up getting a job, having a wife and a spirit-filled church that he attended on a regular basis. He said as long as I lived with Jesus in my heart, life's road would be smooth and with Jesus, we would know how to handle the bumps when they came.

That evening Bob returned with his wife Joan. Joan read out of the Bible for several hours. We sang songs and they asked me if I wanted to ask Jesus to come into my heart! I accepted. Jesus and the Holy Spirit came into my heart. I was born again, amid much repenting, crying, and speaking fluently in tongues and the heavenly language.

Since then, I am most grateful to Bob and Joan Robertson. My life has changed drastically in all areas. I no longer have an inferiority complex due to being legally blind; my language has been cleaned up and does not involve swearing and cussing as before; my urge to gamble has vanished; and many other positive changes happened, too numerous to mention.

I called Bob Robertson on 10/19/07 at his home in Amery, Wisconsin to thank him and Joan for witnessing to me 25 years ago. Bob told me that Joan had gone to be with the Lord about 11 years ago due to cancer. Bob said he was 82 years old and he too had cancer in the spine so I prayed for his healing from his cancer. I let him know that I was most grateful to him and Joan for what they had done for me.

Thank God for these two witnesses!

10. MY TESTIMONY

Jesus put in my heart an urgency to tell others about Him. Shortly after that evening I knew that I should use my experiences as a delivered gambler and a drunk to witness to others in those areas for Jesus Christ. I had nearly gone to prison because of the gambling so Jesus told me to be a witness to prisoners as well. So to this day, of over 25 years later, I have been using those old liabilities as my assets to constantly witness Jesus to gamblers, drunks, homeless, prisoners, and anyone that I come into contact with on a daily basis. Praise God!

I am so glad that Jesus came to me that evening and lifted me out of the miry clay and set my feet on a solid rock and put a new song in my heart! (Psalm 40) I also think of II Corinthians 5:17 that says, "when you accept Jesus into your heart, all the old passes away and everything becomes new!" These scriptures and many others apply to my life. I live today with joy in my heart and know that I have been delivered. I am serving the Lord everyday as I go through life witnessing for Jesus!

Thank you Jesus for coming into my life and saving my soul! I know that my redeemer lives and I know that my name is written down in the book of life! Thank you Jesus!

Bob and Joan Roberts led me in the "Sinner's Prayer" that night. I asked the Lord to come into my life and to live in me and also to be spirit-filled from that point on. I'd like to repeat that so that anyone who is reading this book will, essentially, be able to say the same prayer and, if they're sincere about it, the Lord will come into their heart. The prayer goes like this:

"I Lyn, ask you Jesus, to come into my heart and to live in me from this point forward, to forgive me of all my sins that I have committed, and to wipe the slate totally clean; of all the bad things that I have done. Lord I confess unto You all the things that have been dishonest or corrupt, all the things that are against Your will – all of those things, Lord God, I confess to You, and ask Your forgiveness.

And I pray Jesus, that You'll live in my heart from this day forward and help me to serve You, to do the things I need to do to serve You from this point on. Help me to change my ways, to live honestly for You, to tell the truth and to not be a con-artist. Help me to do things the way that You want me to. And, Jesus, just be with me from this point on and live with me every day so I may not have fear of any collapse, or anything in my life.

Give me strength, oh God, and I thank you for this time and for this prayer, in Jesus' name, Amen."

That was the "Sinner's Prayer," or a form of the "Sinner's Prayer" where you confess all your sins and ask the Lord to remove them, forgive you for them, and then to live in you, to be a servant for Him from that point on. I wanted to mention it because – if anyone is reading this book they can do that same thing and it will be eternally beneficial for them.

I want to speak about the preoccupation of gambling. When gambling, it totally ran my life, from the morning when I woke up to when I went to bed. I thought of nothing else; about how I was going to get money to gamble with, pay bookies, and in general everything about money. It was like I had no time to think of anything else. My mind was so occupied with money issues that I had absolutely no peace of mind. It was terrible. It was like I was trapped in my mind and nothing around me mattered. The only way out of this was to call upon the Lord Jesus. He gave me peace! And He can accomplish the same for you.

I also spent 4 months of my recovery at the Kinnic Falls Halfway House in my early recovery. The House was instrumental in alleviating problems from my old life and renewing my love of the Lord Jesus. The following is a short article that I wrote as I was leaving the halfway house:

CONCEPT OF A HALFWAY HOUSE

At one time, I thought that a halfway house was similar to a junk yard for old, used automobiles; a place where alcoholics and chemically dependent people were placed in an "end of the road" situation. Since residing in a halfway house for a portion of a year, I have found the above concept to be quite untrue. Dissimilar to the junk yard idea, where an auto finds its final resting place and is dismantled for scrap and parts, the halfway house environment gives the human being who has gone astray via alcoholism, chemical dependency, compulsive gambling, or other obsessions an opportunity to restore and rebuild his life on this earth.

Rather than being the "end of the road" for the chemical dependent personality, the halfway house offers a second, third, fourth, or nth chance to the person for the restoration of his spirit and character. This is done primarily by an individual taking a good close look at himself in the atmosphere of the halfway house through group and individual counseling in an attempt to "remove the rust" such as dishonesty, mistrust, unmanageability, and insanity from his life. This is achieved by the individual admitting firmly, his powerlessness over certain specific addictions and accepting that a Power greater than himself can restore him to a normal way of living. A twelve-step program, a prayer of serenity, and a philosophy of living one day at a time, are the tools granted to a person in this program.

Most importantly, the halfway house gives a person an opportunity to get his "spiritual motor" running. The realization for the first time perhaps that an individual can turn his will and life over to the care of a higher power is not only astounding, but once it is truly done gives the highest echelon of serenity and peace of mind achievable. To learn to trust God or an A.A. group removes the worry and fear that has been prevalent in the lives of most chemically dependent people. To love a God or higher power on a day-by-day basis allows a recovering alcoholic to commune with that God daily for inner strength and peace. And finally, to be able to pray and communicate with a higher power on a daily, or as needed basis, and to realize that "All things work together for good for those who believe in a higher power," one can achieve the highest level of sobriety attainable, centered around a sincere spiritual program with fervent faith in a higher power.

Concluding, I am extremely thankful that my God has permitted me to be in a halfway house for a brief portion of my life. There has been a purpose for me here as there is a plan for my entire life on a day-by-day basis. I am especially grateful that my life has been restored to sanity which has been exhibited in the restoration of my family, job, new friends, and my faith in a higher power. I am indeed thankful for my sobriety! So we learn how to pray. We learn how to be in conscious contact with God. And once you're born again, then you have a personal relationship with Jesus.

11. BELIEVING

I don't see physically well, but I can close my eyes and pray through the worldly stuff. Then I get a vision of what the Lord looks like. In my mind I see Him on the cross. I thank God for dying on the cross for me. I observe Him coming out of the tomb. I thank God for coming out of the tomb on Easter Sunday. I thank God for His ascension, when He returned into heaven 40 days later. I'm envisioning the Holy Spirit coming down on Pentecost 50 days after Easter. Also I set inner eyes on another picture where I see the Lord Jesus riding on a cloud coming this way. That tells my heart that it's not too long from now when the Rapture Day will be here.

About the Rapture; it is written in I Thessalonians 4:16-18. "With a shout, and with the voice of the Arch Angel, Jesus Christ will descend from heaven, and the dead in Christ will rise first, all of those people who have believed in Jesus and died on this earth will rise and be united with a glorified body and go with the Lord."

So, with a shout and with a voice of the Arch Angel, and with the trump of God, Jesus Christ will descend from heaven and all of the dead in Christ will rise first, and all of those who are living that believe in Jesus Christ will be caught up in the air to live with the Lord there forever after. And it says in verse 18 that we are to comfort each other with these sayings until the day of the Rapture. And the people (myself included) have plans.

I have no doubt about it that I'm going to heaven when the Lord comes. It's really firm in my mind. I see my name written in the Book of Life, which also happens when you say the Sinner's Prayer and ask

God to come into your life. As we go up on Rapture Day, we'll go to the first large event that will take place, and that will be the Wedding Feast where the Lord Jesus will be united with His church, the church that has been waiting on earth here to be brought up to heaven. And it will be a large dinner banquet, a wedding feast banquet.

As a mathematician, I've looked many times at the size of heaven. It's a cube, 1,500 miles on a side; that is, 1,500 miles high, 1,500 miles wide, and 1,500 miles long. It's a cube that has that much space (approximately 3,375,000,000 cubic miles which is 3 billion, 375 million cubic miles) in it. I think about it, and almost lose myself. How long is the table going to be at the wedding feast, with all the people? The dead in Christ will be arriving first. All the living Christians will be caught up in the air after that. It's a mind-boggling, glorious matter, thinking about such an event.

And for those who do not come up in the Rapture, they will be left on earth to begin what's called the "Tribulation Period." And the Tribulation Period is a period of time on earth when all the police force and people who are trying to do right will be removed from this earth. And crime and sin and everything will just run wild. You think it's bad now when you turn on the TV and listen to all the murders and the stealing and the rapes and all the other things that are going on? It'll be a hundredfold then. You won't be safe going out of your house because your neighbor will probably want to shoot you for the things you have in your house. So, it's not going to be any fun if you're left behind in the Rapture. And there's a whole series of books that my wife Rosie has read about being "Left Behind," They tell about the situation and how you don't want to be left behind. You want to be home with the Lord Jesus, having Him in your heart. This is a real hope.

The reason why I write this book is that whoever reads it would be inspired to turn to the Lord Jesus and be saved. They can, by simply saying the Sinner's Prayer and going to a Bible believing, Bible preaching Christian church. At such a church, with a sincere pastor you can be assured that if you give your life to the Savior, that you will be in the good graces of the Lord Jesus, and you will have a personal relationship with Him. It's these things that we learn about when we read the Bible, and we fortify our faith with knowing what's going to happen.

At the end of the Tribulation, which is a seven-year period, will come the second coming of the Lord where all of the Christians will follow Him on white horses and the Lord will be first with eyes of fire and a Sword in his mouth and the Battle of Armageddon will occur in Jerusalem and with one swath of the Lord's sword the enemy; terrorists, all Satan's people, and all evil will be defeated. Blood will run out of Jerusalem 20 feet deep for 200 miles. Another similar account is as follows. At the Wedding Feast for the seven-year period, and, at the end of the seven-year period, the Lord will come riding on a white horse, not the God of love and concern that you all think of, but this will be a God with fiery red in his eyes, with a sword in his mouth, with a long flowing sash on a white horse, and all of us Christians will be on white horses, dressed in white, following Him as well. And this will be forecast in the sky for several months over Israel showing the Lord Jesus coming and all His followers, for the battle of Armageddon.

And the battle will happen in Israel and all of the world forces, all of the terrorists, all of the crooks, all of the mafia, all of those who are of Satan's camp, all of Satan's angels and demons and warriors will prepare to do battle with the Lord Jesus. The Lord will return during the second coming and, with one swat of the sword, will kill all of the evil people that are on earth, all of the people, and the blood will run so thick out of Jerusalem at that point that it's said to be six feet deep of nothing but red blood flowing out of Jerusalem where all of the evil people have been killed by the Lord. And I can think of nothing better than being on the Lord's side at that juncture, and being on Lord Jesus Christ's side. The devil will also be thrown into a bottomless pit shortly thereafter, and he will be locked there for 1,000 years, and an angel will throw him in there and lock him in and keep the key for that 1,000 year period.

During that time, the Christians will set up a new world here on earth and the new world will be run by those that the Lord Jesus appoints to do different jobs. It's oftentimes said that the people who are high up in this world, the CEOs and the other people, if they're Christian people, will be the people that will be dumping the trash cans and sweeping the floors and things like that, because what the Lord has said is that those who have been first here will be last in heaven, and vice-versa. Those who have been last here will be first in heaven. This is in store, we'll do that for 1,000 years, and then Satan will be loosed again for a brief period of time where he will cause a lot of turmoil. This will lead to the White Throne Judgment a short time after that, where all of the bodies of people that have died will be brought up for final judgment, all of the bodies at the bottom of the sea, all of the bodies that have been murdered or broken into pieces by Hurricane Katrina, or any other bad storm will be brought up and will be placed before the White Throne Judgment that God himself will conduct. And, at this point, there will be one last chance for people to say the Sinner's Prayer, and ask Jesus Christ to come into their heart, and this will be the time where people, if they do not do this – if they resist, if they refuse, if they keep thinking it's baloney, they will be thrown into the Lake of Fire, where they will live in misery forever and ever, where nothing but bad things happen, nothing but burning everything that they will do will be complete misery for them and they will wish, wish, wish that they had made a different decision at the White Throne Judgment. Those at the White Throne Judgment that decide that they want to ask Jesus to come into their life by saying the Sinner's Prayer or answering the altar call that God gives will be allowed to be with the Christians and to live with the Lord Jesus and God in heaven from that point on. Praise God! Praise God! Praise God!

Here is The Sinner's Prayer! Please say it out loud and ask Jesus Christ to come into your life today and save your soul forever and ever!

I, _____, ask You, Jesus Christ, to forgive me of all my sins (past and present). Remove them from me and bury them at the bottom of the sea. I confess all my sins that I have ever committed and I know that You are faithful and just to forgive me. I ask you to come into my heart right now and to love me and live in me from this day forth.

Dear Jesus, I promise to serve you all the days of my earthly life and I look forward to spending eternity with you in heaven!

If you have just said the Sinner's Prayer, you should get a copy of the Holy Bible and begin reading in the book of John in the New Testament. Call and go to a full gospel church such as an Assembly of God Church or a Church of God (Cleveland, TN) Church. Talk to the pastor at that church and he will help you with prayer and meditation for worshipping Jesus on a daily basis. Attend church services and get involved in ministry activities of the church to serve the Lord! Make certain the church you choose is a full gospel church and one that you have a direct line to Jesus without having to go through a priest, preacher, or minister to get to Him! The Bible says the only way to get to God is through Jesus Christ! There is no other way. Your life will become truly blessed and you will live a rich and fruitful life. Praise God! Thank you Jesus! Thank you Jesus for saving my soul!

To continue looking at the last days; the evil prophets and the witnesses, and all of the different bad things that are talked about with regard to the dragon and so forth, they'll all be thrown into the Lake of Fire and Sulfur. The devil himself will be thrown in as the final one, and they'll stay there from that point on forever and ever and ever. Whereas, the people that made the decision to follow Jesus Christ will live in that large cube 1,500 miles by 1,500 miles by 1,500 miles, and they'll be having a wonderful time with the Lord Jesus. The River of Life will run through heaven with the Tree of Knowledge on each side of the river. The Tree will bear a different kind of fruit for every month of the year from that point on. So, it's extremely beneficial to be able to recognize that we have an opportunity to live there! There is hope available in this crazy old world with regard to everything that's going on. The only hope in this world is to know Jesus Christ and have Him as your personal Savior. This is the time to do it.

Make sure the church you pick is full gospel, because there are a lot of fakes in the last days. Once you've asked the Lord to come into your life, you then have a strong desire, to every day read the Bible and pray, and have a personal relationship with Jesus Christ. You learn to desire to pray about everything. The Bible (Basic Instructions Before Leaving Earth) says we should pray continually. This comes from reading his Word and applying it to one's life. As it says in the Bible, "You have to draw nigh onto God before He will draw nigh onto you." In other words, God does not automatically show up. He loves you very much, but you have to call Him up (through prayer) and seek Him. It says the same in Step 11 of the recovery program: "sought through prayer and meditation; to improve my conscious contact with God, praying for knowledge of His will for me, and the power to carry that out." So, we have to seek Him. Seek and you will find as it says in the Word. Stay in the Word of God on a daily basis.

Today when my wife read the devotion to me the topic was "Loving Your Enemies." That means not being bitter, or carrying hatred, but loving your enemies and doing good to them, no matter what the situation is in life. If we are upset with other people, or they have done us wrong, we are to love them. Reading the Bible, reminds us how to make our lives better.

I am growing closer to God every day. I end up praying for whatever I do throughout the day, as it says in the 24-hour book for AA and also in the Bible, "Keep praying and don't stop praying." The guides to my life are the promises in the Bible. I resort back to the Ten Commandments and Exodus 20 frequently. The Ten Commandments that were given by God to Moses on the top of the mountain are still basic rules by which we live and can have a good Christian life.

12. TEN COMMANDMENTS

Here are the 10 commandments for living right! God says:

I. I am the Lord thy God, thou shall not have any gods before me.

II. Thou shall not take the Lord's name in vain. The Lord will not hold him guiltless who takes His name in vain.

III. Remember the Sabbath day and keep it holy.

IV. Honor your father and mother that your days may be long upon the land which the Lord thy God gives you.

V. Thou shall not kill.

VI. Thou shall not commit adultery.

VII. Thou shall not steal.

VIII. Thou shall not bare false witness against your neighbor.

IX. Thou shall not covet your neighbor's wife.

X. Thou shall not covet anything that belongs to your neighbor.

Commandment One says, "I am the Lord thy God. Thou shall have no other Gods before me." And that's telling us that God is God, and there's no one else. Buddha, Confucius, and Muhammad – all these other gods that claim they're the same thing – it is not like that. Not all rivers run into one, as some people say. Some individuals who try to be kind to others say, "Hey, you'll get there by going this route." That's not the case because it says in the Word of God the only way to get to the Father is through Jesus Christ. That is the only approach that works, to have contact with God Almighty, God Omnipotent and God All Present and the Creator of the World. As Commandment One says, "I am the Lord thy God. Thou shall have no other Gods before me." And we cannot make money or materialistic things a god in our lives. I had that problem way back when, but I've gotten over it now and I put God first in what I am doing. We put God first. It's a matter of obeying on a daily basis.

Commandment Two says, "Thou shall not take the Lord thy God's name in vain for the Lord will not hold him guiltless whoever takes His name in vain." One thing we need to do is to clean up our vocabulary and language when we become Christians. We should not blaspheme, or do anything with bad language. We must go throughout the day with a clean mouth and clean thoughts. I know this Commandment helped me to remedy swearing and dishonest thoughts so that I would have a cleaner verbal expression at all times. I'm thankful for Commandment Two. When I accepted Jesus in the Sinner's Prayer, I noticed immediately that my mouth no longer had bad words coming from it.

Commandment Three says, "Remember the Sabbath Day to keep it holy." This is the day that God set aside. He worked six days creating the earth and on the seventh, God rested. This is what we are to do too. Work six days and rest on the seventh. The business world does not obey this law for it is open 24, 7 throughout the year. They will have to answer to God for this.

The Fourth Commandment is as follows: "Honor thy father and thy mother so that your days may be long upon the land that the Lord thy God giveth thee." And this Commandment states that if you obey your parents as you're growing up you'll have a long life; I can attest to that. The Word of God says if you obey you will be blessed.

We had a neighbor, Jean Patton, at our condo where we lived in Tucson. She was around 95 years old, and very spry. I would tell her. "Jean, you must've obeyed your parents when you were a child, growing up."

She'd answer, "Yeah, I did. I didn't have any problem with that. My mother and father were both strict, but I learned to obey them."

"That's probably no doubt why you have a long life," I said. "You continue on doing the things that you're doing."

Obeying and having a godly home is very important with regard to a father, mother and children in the home, and this is what is put forth in Commandment Four.

Commandment Five says "thou shall not kill." This is something you definitely do not want to do as a Christian. Today's world has gone astray because of all the killings and murders. If you turn on the news you will hear that someone else has been killed or wiped out. A person has to have some rules to live by, to actually guide one's life. A most important rule is not to take other people's lives. It is even hard for me to think about killing an animal now; where as in my early days, I used to enjoy hunting. That's something I don't want to do anymore. If a person harbors hatred in his heart for another person, this is a form of murder and it too breaks the Fifth Commandment.

Commandment Six is, "Thou shall not commit adultery." When you are a man and a wife, you have a sexual relationship, and it's meant to be. When you are happily married, that is meant to be. Extra sexual activity involving unmarried people, shacking up with someone else's spouse, sexual activity among 2 or more men, or 2 or more women, orgies between groups of men and women – all these are against God's rules according to Commandment Six. So again, if you obey you'll be blessed. If you do not commit adultery, you'll be blessed.

If you lose your mate, God will give you a new one. This will allow you to have free expression of your love for each other (man and wife).

Immoral sexual activity is rampant in our society. If you don't understand what I'm talking about, turn on your TV and listen to which governor or politician is having an extramarital affair. The world is loaded with mega sexual activity (becoming the fashionable thing to do) and it is totally against God's will. It's another sign that we are in the last days, and the Rapture is soon to occur. Also if a man looks at a woman lusting after her and desiring to have sex with her, Commandment Six has been violated in God's eyes. This is also if a woman looks at a man and desires to have sex with him. Obey these commandments and be blessed!

Commandment Seven, "Thou shall not steal." There's too much outward and inward theft that goes on in this world. Again, as a Christian you're guided by this commandment. If you see things in a store that you would like to have, you don't try and sneak it into your pocket or shoplift it. In this day and age, there's so much theft going on with regard to personal identity; people's social security numbers are being found or stolen and used. There's also extortion in the white-collar level. Heads of companies are ripping off and stealing from their employees and their own companies. Enron was a good example of that with CEOs taking advantage of the workers and shareholders, for their own glamour, greed and good.

Also employees' stealing from their employers on the job is a breaking of Commandment Seven. When they leave at noon and claim they are working until 5 p.m., then 5 hours have been stolen from the company. Taking writing pads, pens, or staplers from the office file cabinet for personal reasons is stealing by the employee from the employer. Again turn to the news channels on TV and you'll see many examples of stealing and breaking of the seventh Commandment. The world is loaded with people driven by greed and fame who steal, cheat, and step over others when climbing the corporate ladder! Commandment Seven is very important to live by in this day and age. The righteous (those close to God) will be rewarded with a home in heaven!

The Eighth Commandment says, "Thou shall not bear false witness against thy neighbor." It seems that everybody lies about others. You do not want to be gossiping or saying bad things but to love and be good to thy neighbor. This goes for people at work; it goes for those you are acquainted with, and folks in church as well. It is your responsibility to be friendly and generally get along well with other people. Your neighbor is anyone that you come in contact with. We must love our neighbor as ourselves.

Commandment Nine says, "Thou shall not covet thy neighbor's wife." And, again if you're a man and happily married, you don't have a desire to be with your neighbor's wife, even though she may be very attractive. You do not go to bed with her, even if it is only in your mind. You greet her as a neighbor and are kind to her on a neighborly basis. In other words, if you have a wife that doesn't do certain things, and you have a neighbor's wife that does certain things, you don't want to covet that. Basically, you just want to have your own, get along as best you can and maybe you can show your present wife just exactly what you would like to have done and it may improve. So, it's very good.

And, Commandment Ten, is also, "Thou shall not covet anything that belongs to your neighbors," like cars, snowmobiles, vacation homes, or anything that might cause greed or lust. As Christians we should be happy with what we have and be content with what we have for getting along. In Romans, we are told to be content with whatever our situation is.

The Ten Commandments are a guide to all Christians. Even though the world refutes it, as a Christian person who believes that you're going to heaven, it's imperative that you run your life by the rules of the Ten Commandments and other promises in the Bible.

We must continue to witness Jesus to this dying world, one person at a time. The Lord says, "The harvest is WHITE, and the workers are few." We must continue to witness Jesus to the world and enlist other people to help also.

13. BIBLE PROMISES

An example of a Bible promise is in Malachi 3:10, the last book in the Old Testament. It says that, "If you bring all of the tithes," (a tithe is one-tenth of what you make) "into the storehouse, God will open the windows of heaven and pour out blessings to you 30-fold, 60-fold, 100-fold, so much that you will not be able to contain what He pours out to you."

If you're bringing a tenth of the grain into the storehouse the bag that you bring it in will be running over; it'll not be big enough to contain all of the contents that God will give you in return. So, this is the promise; if you bring the tithes into the storehouse, then God will open the windows of heaven and pour out blessings to you more than you can hold...not just materialistic but blessings of joy, fruitfulness, good health, friendliness...all kinds of blessings.

And every day, I feel like I'm totally blessed from the top of my head to the bottom of my feet, and that's the blessings that God has given back to me, being a born again, spirit filled Christian! Materialistic goods come when you do not even expect it to come.

There are so many promises in the Word of God for the born again, spirit filled Christian who has a desire to read God's Word daily, to pray continuously and go to church to worship with other Christians. These promises are very important (as well as praising and thanking God) to those who have a personal relationship with Him.

A couple other Bible verses come to my mind that I've stood on for many years. I was given this verse by someone at a non-denominational church: Philippians 4:6 and 7 *"Do not worry about anything. Ask God what you need, be thankful for what you have, and God will give you a peace that passes all human understanding."* That verse seemed to make good sense to me, with all my problems. It told me, "Don't worry about anything. Enjoy the moment that you have. Ask God for what you need."

Asking God in prayer for whatever you need, or to get you over the next hump is very important. Be thankful for what you have. Be thankful for what God has given you. Thank Him for all the blessings of family, of materialistic things, of clothes to wear, of air to breathe, and having hope in your heart. Be thankful for that and God will give you a peace that passes all human understanding. This peace runs in my life from day to day. I just feel totally content, for God has given me complete peace. Many times in my early recovery, and still today I will say *Philippians 4:6 and 7, "Do not worry about anything, ask God what you need, be thankful for what you have, and God will give you a peace that passes all human understanding."*

A sister verse to this, that I often repeat, is from Proverbs 3:5, 6, *"Trust in the Lord with all your heart and lean not on your own understanding. Acknowledge him in all your ways, and He will direct your path."*

In other words, if we trust in the Lord, whatever happens to us (bad or good), will be turned over to Jesus, like Step 3 in the recovery program. Dear God, I turn the will of my life over to Your care. Do with me whatever You want. I trust in You oh Lord, with all my heart and lean not on my own understanding. In Jesus' name I pray. Amen.

My understanding is limited. I have a certain level of understanding about why this should be done or why it should not be done but if I trust in the Lord and go beyond that and simply don't think about my own understanding, then Jesus will take care of it, and will bring it to conclusion in His timing. I just thank God for that. It says, *"Trust in the Lord with all your heart, lean not on your own understanding. Acknowledge him in all you do,"* which is important too.

Whatever I do during the day if I pray ahead of time "God help me with this," "Be with me as I do that," it helps me to make it though. If I thank God for being with me and helping me when I'm done, I have a conclusion to it and peace in my heart as well. And the very last part says, *"He will direct our paths."* Doing these things; trusting and acknowledging Him in all our ways and not leaning on our own understanding, guarantees that He *will* direct our paths. The steps of a righteous man are ordered, as it says in the Word of God. My steps *are* ordered, and the steps of any Christian who believes are ordered. I take one step at a time. God knows where I'm going next.

As I write this, I'm currently in between grants of research at the Arizona Cancer Center. I just spent five years doing prostate cancer research, and NPC research, Niemann-Pick C disease for dying children. And, after a five-year period, the NIH, National Institute of Health, decided not to fund the grant again. So, I'm in between doing that and looking for another position at the University of Arizona, University of Hawaii, or wherever God might be leading me. I pray for His direction, and pray that He will let me know where He wants me to be through telephone, email, or however He chooses. I just rely on Him. I trust in Him during this time, even standing in a grocery line, James 5:7, "Be patient." Allow someone to go ahead of you, that has just one or two articles, if you have half a basket of items; that is a way of showing love.

Living a Christian life has been very fruitful for m, and having a Christian wife is wonderful as well. I prayed for my wife. Being a visually-impaired person, I cannot see well enough to pick out a lady whom I wanted to date and get to know. I prayed, and God brought me Rose. This was a blessing in itself.

14. BREAKUP OF A HOME

In 1989 I had been in recovery for seven years. My wife Jean had been going to Gam-Anon and Al-Anon during that time as well. She announced to me one day that she wanted a divorce because the emotional pain of the gambling was still with her and bothered her. I talked to her several times about getting rid of that and told her that as Christians, we should not break up. Jean had been from a Catholic background and I had been from a Protestant background. She mentioned to me a couple times that I was much stronger in my faith with God than she was, so she wanted our children to be raised according to my Protestant religion. Both Mark and Stephanie were raised in a Lutheran church with the traditional Lutheran upbringing.

In 1989, Jean explained to me that the emotional pain of the gambling, how it affected all the neighbors and relatives there in River Falls, Wisconsin was too much, that she had to get out of the marriage and the relationship. Pleading and begging with her did not work. She said she had to divorce me. She went through the process of divorce through attorneys and so forth. Finally, late in 1989, early 1990, we were divorced and legally separated with the dividing up of our home and possessions. She continued living in the home with our two children and I lived down the street in a condominium where I could walk over to my office at the University. I am very thankful that I had strong relationships with AA and GA people, along with my church friends, to help me through this low period.

The breakup was a sad time in my life. As a Christian, I didn't want it to happen. But she divorced me and there was nothing I could do about it, other than accept it. I called her many times and asked if there was a possibility of getting back together but she was firm in her decision. I found myself saying the Serenity Prayer many times and very often. The Serenity Prayer goes this way, *God grant me serenity to accept the things I cannot change, courage to change the things I can, and wisdom to know the difference!*

Now as I look back at it several years later, I am reminded of the Old Testament instruction that a man and a woman should be equally yoked in their marriage. That was not the case in our marriage. Equally yoked means that a man and woman are one spiritually, and that they believe in God the same way and that they are one person in the Lord! They read and believe in the Bible, pray together, and lift each other up when needed. In other words, we were not of one kin, we were not of one spirit because of her upbringing, and mine. There was always a difference with our thinking and in our spiritual life, even though she had consented to raise the children in the Lutheran tradition. And she continued to go to the Lutheran church for a time, even after the divorce. Anyway, that taught me a lesson about being equally yoked with the woman I'm married to. Both men and women should be equally yoked, or of one kin, one spirit. They become one, as the Bible says, one flesh and one spirit. That was a rough time because of the loss of a 21 year long relationship.

I now pray for my former wife, Jean. I thank God for our good times and the children we had together. I am grateful for the memory of playing bridge and numerous weekend nights dancing together to old-time music, like polkas and waltzes at the Bay City Ballroom and Proch's Popular Ballroom. There were many occasions we spent together, dancing and enjoying the old-time music. We attended various wedding dances for friends and relatives, and both cried our hearts out when the Bay City Ballroom burned to the ground. For a long time we were sad because we had so many enjoyable times there. I still remember, yet today. God bless you Jean, for all of the good times we had together. Thank you! I am thankful that she married again and this time to a Catholic man, so their chances of being equally yoked would be far better.

I would see my son and my daughter during the week, and so forth and it always broke me up internally to not be able to go home with them to the nice home that we had on the corner at 1210 E. Golf View

Drive there in River Falls, Wisconsin. It was not to be, so time moved on in a different direction.

It was at this time that I met another woman in A.A. It turned out to be a bad situation because she was still using and I had about 7 years of sobriety. She was still a closet drinker and I did not recognize it for quite awhile. I'm not going to elaborate on this because it is not worth repeating, but with the help of Cam-Anon (a sister program to GA) and help from church friends, I was finally able to put an end to our friendship once and for all! Thank God!

The lesson to be learned here is that if you are early in recovery from any addiction; do not start a relationship with someone of the opposite sex before that person has at least two years of being clean from the addiction. I'm writing this book to help people live a better life! I had to learn the hard way and then make the correction for my own life and program of recovery. I thank God that I did not lose my own recovery from alcoholism and compulsive gambling during this time, that I was able to stay clean and sober. Thank God!

15. STEPHANIE GOES TO BE WITH JESUS

It is difficult for me to write about my lovely daughter. A couple years after the divorce, in 1991, a tragedy occurred that added to the misery and to the despair that I was going through. My daughter, Stephanie, was fatally injured in a car accident in 1991 on a Friday evening. Stephanie and I had been exceptionally close. She would come to my office at the University many days after school. We were devoted to each other, father and daughter. Even after the divorce she would still stop by almost every day, and we would talk. I would give her money for a treat from the vending machine and she'd get a candy bar upstairs. She'd come back down and we would talk about her school, friends, and everything dads and daughters talk about when they are together. She'd read the Bible to me and from a Portals of Prayer devotion book that I kept in my office. I always kept the Bible near me, ever since I had been born again and spirit filled.

This particular Friday night she was in my office after school and mentioned that she was going to stay overnight with Christa and a couple other girls (all were 15), and would see me tomorrow morning. I remember that we read the Bible and prayed together while at my office. She had both parents approval, as she had frequently done before. It was late afternoon when Steph gave me a hug and said "Dad, I'll see you in the morning."

She left my office, informing me that Jean was going to give her a ride to Christa's house in the early evening. I finished my work and walked from my office to South Fork café and had the Friday Fish Fry. Then I went to the upper A.A. meeting and talked to my friends before walking home to my condo. I remember while walking, thinking how close I was to both my children, Mark and Steph, and how blessed I was to have two such wonderful kids. I still could not believe that divorce had occurred in my family. I remember entering the condo, watching a little T.V., and going to bed with a peaceful mind.

Steph and two other girls went to spend the night at Christa's house. The next morning, the doorbell rang at my place about 6:30 a.m. I came downstairs and there was a police officer standing at the door. He brought the news to me that my daughter had been fatally injured in a car accident and would not be coming home.

I was devastated. The anger boiled up inside me, and I exploded with all kinds of emotions. Fortunately, the hopes of my spiritual program was still there because, as I did every day, I opened the shades and raised my arms and thanked God for His grace to me that day, and for His free unmerited love. Even though that was a real tough, tough thing on that particular day, I still did it. The policeman hugged me (we knew each other years ago from town), and just consoled me as best he could. I talked to the pastor that afternoon about several different things. I felt so sad and lost I could hardly stand it. Then my son, Mark, came in my door crying his eyes out and angry as all get out. He hugged me and cried out and said, "Everything has gone bad: divorce, and now this terrible thing!" Mark and Steph were very close as brother and sister. Mark was 20 years old and Steph was 15 when this occurred. Mark and I hugged each other and cried together all day. I love my son too.

Jean had been in the Twin Cities at a hospital all night until Steph went home to be with Jesus about 2:30 a.m. on October 12, 1991. She was born on September 11, 1976 and had been part of our family since September 28, 1976. Steph was a beautiful girl with a gentle and kind spirit about her.

Friends and neighbors up and down our street, Wasson Lane, came over to my place and to Jean's house all day and week. My former wife, and mother to Steph, was just as devastated as I, and was crying all the time as well. We hugged each other and cried in each other's shoulders!

We found out later that the 4 girls decided to take Christa's parents car out for a joy ride around midnight (they were all 15 and no one had a driver's license) on some of the old roads west of River Falls. They were driving too fast and the car flipped over, head first, and came down hard right where Stephanie was sitting buckled in the front seat passenger's side. She was fatally injured but the other three had only minor cuts and bruises. What a lot of grief, heartache, and legal tangle caused by four teenage girls at a slumber party! It changed the course of everyone's lives from that point.

A Christian and long time friend of the family, Randy Cudd, gave me a ride to the St. Paul City Morgue on Saturday where I identified my daughter's body. What a contrast from 24 hours earlier at my office to this! I stood there and prayed for our family that we would be able to make it in its divorced state and now the loss of our precious daughter… Dear Jesus, please help us make it just one moment at a time. After about 45 minutes, we left the morgue and Randy drove me home to River Falls back to my condo. He prayed with me, he was a solid Christian brother. I remain thankful to Randy Cudd for all his help and prayers during this very tough time.

Later that day it was a trip to Cashman's Funeral Home and Greenwood Cemetery in River Falls for the funeral and burial arrangements. The following day was Sunday so we all went to Ezekiel Lutheran Church (where our family worshipped) with heavy hearts. We received compassionate condolences from friends and the fellowship of the Church.

The funeral was the next day at Ezekiel Lutheran Church. The church was overflowing with people and students from Steph's high school. People and students (about 500) and the whole church body were in attendance. What a contrast from a few hours before on Friday afternoon in my office where Steph and I talked and laughed and enjoyed each other's company with Bible reading and prayer, to now as I looked at her in the casket all quiet and peaceful.

I knew she was with Jesus because she had told me Friday afternoon prior that she loved Jesus and someday she would be with the Lord. So as her dad, I knew and believed she was with Jesus. However, the grief and sadness of her loss was so strong that all I could do was cry.

When everyone was settled in the church, the casket was brought in. Jean, Mark and I, arm in arm together, hugging each other, crying our eyes out, followed the casket to the front of the church. Full concentration was on Steph so I did not hear much of the sermon and the hymns that were sung. The recessional took place and we followed the hearse to Greenwood Cemetery where the burial took place. This was a very sad affair but the words of the minister gave me hope that Steph would be raised to life on the day of the Lord! I believed that and I was reminded of I Thessalonians 4:16-18, "*With a shout and the trump of God, Jesus will descend from heaven and the dead in Christ will rise first.*" Therefore, I knew that for eternity sake, Steph was okay and on solid ground! Praise God! Praise God! Thank you Jesus!

The following week Jean and I picked out a heart shaped gravestone with a small picture of Steph on it toward the bottom. The stone was erected on Steph's gravesite later that week. A favorite saying that Steph had was also engraved into her gravestone. It says: "You can do nothing about the length of your life, but you can do something about the width and depth of your life!" All of us were in deep mourning and heavy grieving for weeks thereafter.

16. HEALING

I was totally devastated, and the divorce, followed by Steph's death, really tested my spiritual walk with God. The loss of two fundamental family relationships was crucial. I must admit it, my faith wavered at times, you know: Why did this happen? What for? What's going on here? My walk really deviated, but it seemed like something kept strong all the way through, knowing that God had a plan for my life. It was just a real tough thing for the next two years. We would get a bit of positive news if a legal decision went our way. It was a lot of brooding and a lot of misery with regard to how we get over this, how we move ahead. Times passing began to heal us slowly, day by day.

Divorce and Stephanie's death were especially hard on my son, Mark, because he was extremely close to his sister and he had real bouts of depression and anger and had to see clergy, counselors, and the like to help to keep his head on right. He was a junior in college when this took place. Finally, it was suggested to Mark that he should be a Big Brother to a little boy and this would help him and it did. Mark's little boy was Anthony and he did not have a dad. Helping Anthony really helped Mark immensely and it was good for both of them. Mark would update me on what he was doing with Anthony from time to time. This Big Brother program worked great! A little later, Mark met Nancy who later became his girlfriend. So things began to get better for my son with two new people in his life. I was happy about this because I love my son and wanted the best for him.

For me being a member of Alcoholic Anonymous, and Gamblers Anonymous, some people in those groups mentioned I could go to a group called "Compassionate Friends," which was a group of parents who had lost children. So, I went to a couple meetings in St. Paul, Minnesota, and it was really a different group. I remember one night there was 75 parents in the room at this Lutheran church and each one had lost a child, or two children. And when they told their story I felt it was excruciating how kids had died. And after the second meeting, I told myself I could not go there anymore because the stories were so damaging, even though it *was* good to share and talk about it. Kids were run over by tractors, caught in machines, shot, hung, all that kind of stuff. It was tremendously tough to sit and listen to all that, knowing that your daughter had passed away, in the manner she did in the accident. So anyway, it was a real difficult time. But I know God was with me through it all.

And finally when I got my head on sometime around 1992, I found myself feeling a great deal of gratitude from the grieving of Stephanie. I was thankful that she'd been with me for 15 years. I kept in mind that she had been adopted. As I explained before we adopted a child because of the chance of having a child that would be born totally blind. And I turned the gratitude into thankfulness and just was appreciative that she was with us for 15 years. And yes, she could have died at age 6, or age 9, or age 13, or at a much earlier age. I would not have had as much time with her as I did. I reminded myself that she had read the Bible to me before she died, and she was born again and spirit-filled as well. So, I have no doubt that she is with Jesus. In fact whenever we sing, "We are standing on holy ground I know that there are angels all around…", I see Steph with angelic clothes on, with Mother and Dad, and Uncle Norris, and all the people that have passed on before us, and I see her mingling with us when we are at church.

It was probably about a year after Stephanie had passed away that I went to the usual Wednesday night service at the Eastside Assembly of God church. I had been having a rough day of grieving the loss of a daughter, a beautiful daughter. She had been lovely, both physically and spiritually, and a delightful daughter for a dad to have. I had gone to the church with a heavy heart that night.

When I arrived I sat toward the front so I could see like I usually do. Pastor Bill Seal was preaching the message that night, and he was preaching about mountaintop experiences. He said that when we leave church we should depart as different people than when we came. He gave as an example Moses going up on the mountain to receive the Ten Commandments from God. Moses came down a changed person. His face showed the glory of God, that he had been in contact with God.

This is what Pastor Bill was talking about to all of us at church that night. However we came in, we should leave different when we go out. At the conclusion of his message, as usual, we had time for prayer at the altar. I was in a kneeling position and in prayer, asking Jesus about Stephanie. "How is she doing?" "What's happening?" "What's going on?"

I really was in essence, complaining a little bit about how miserable I felt and had been feeling over the last couple weeks. I continued to pray. And then I had a vision that my daughter, Stephanie came and stood beside me. She had on a long green gown with an extended brown staff in her hand. She was very beautiful, with her red hair, and a golden crown on her head with three jewels. She had a gentle smile and putting her hand on my shoulder she said, "Dad, don't worry about me at all. I'm with the Lord Jesus in heaven, and it's a real wonderful place. I'll wait till you get here. I'll be with you when you get here. Just be content. Don't worry about me. I'm with Jesus and everything is fine here. You just keep going on with your life there, and don't be worrying about me at all."

I thought her smile sparkled joy at me. "By the way," she continued, "when you go back to Wisconsin to dedicate the Light of Life Memorial outside of my school, tell my friends and neighbors that I'm in heaven, and that everything is just wonderful here, and that they should aspire to go to heaven after they pass away from earth."

She wrapped her arms around me and said, "Dad, don't worry about me."

It was like she reassured me not to worry about anything. Ask God, whatever you need. When I was through praying after 10 or 15 minutes I stood up. The heavy load of the grieving was gone; I felt complete peace that my daughter had come to visit me in that vision. It's been wonderful since that particular time. I've had zero grieving, just no grieving at all.

I think of Stephanie, of her with that same long, green gown, brown staff, jewels in her crown, a big smile, and the peace that she gave me through her voice that evening. So, the heaviness was lifted from my heart and I did leave the church much different than when I came in. It was such a relief after that because I had no basic grieving from that point on.

I think of Stephanie now, I think of her in that picture – with the long, green gown, the brown staff, the crown with the jewels, and the big smile. God did me a huge favor that night by lifting the grieving from me, removing it totally and giving me peace in my mind. So again when we sing, "We are standing on holy ground, I know that there are angels all around..." I see Stephanie amongst those angels, and I see many other people and a lot of other angels. I am looking forward to joining them.

It was a glorious, breathtaking, wonderful time. It helped me to deal, to move on through that particularly hard time. The breakdown of the family with a divorce and the actual death following was a challenging, harsh twosome to handle. My faith remained strong and I was able to continue, especially with the help of the vision on that Wednesday evening at Eastside Assembly in Tucson, Arizona.

17. PROSTATE CANCER PROJECT

I don't remember just exactly what year it was that I was split between the University of Wisconsin, teaching the fall term, to the University of Arizona. It was during this time Dr. Strerioff told me, during one of my kidney transplant evaluations that I should find some sand to walk on in the wintertime rather than ice and snow, because of the 15 year length of the anti-rejection medication. He said, "You're starting to get a little brittle bone structure. Rather than falling on ice and snow and breaking a bone, (which won't heal very fast), it'd be best if you'd find the sunshine of a warm state where there's soft ground to land on or, sand to pile into."

I taught the fall term in Wisconsin (at least for a few years), then would get on a plane and head south. It was in the '70's that I visited my mother in Tucson, Arizona. It was beautiful there, with warm weather, welcoming sunshine, lovely flowers, and palm trees gently waving in the air. I thought it was perfect. In fact the first time I went there, I thought I had died and gone to heaven because it was so delightful, so wonderful coming from the cold and below-zero temperatures with a wind chill of below-zero back in the Midwest, to 75, 78 degrees on a sunny day in February in Tucson. So once he mentioned "find some sand to walk on," I knew exactly where I was going to go and had an opportunity to do just that, through obtaining a visiting scholar position in a statistics program at the University of Arizona.

I actually did it for the spring term of 1991 when the UW-RF granted me a leave of absence. Another visiting professor, Dr. Roger Johnson, who was from the University of Colorado, and I were assigned

74

to teach a basic statistics course to 800 nursing students. Roger did the lecture to the large group in a big auditorium on campus. I had never seen such a large class of young ladies (with a few guys sprinkled in) at one time. I did the small groups lecture and discussion with about 50 students. Roger and I really enjoyed this teaching twosome and we had a lot of fun with the students. What a blast we had doing this teaching for the summer of 1991. I got to know Roger and his wife Tinsia and their son. I taught them and one other the game of bridge. We enjoyed several hours of eating fish and playing bridge. I've visited them in Colorado on several occasions since that initial meeting.

I went back again to Wisconsin after the visiting scholarship and had another kidney transplant evaluation. I told Dr. Sterioff, "I've so much gratitude in my heart for being on dialysis, then being able to get off of it. I've a great deal of appreciation for this place. So what can I do to give back to Mayo Clinic?"

He said, "Well, we have a number of different projects, most of which you couldn't do because of your impaired vision. But there is one that you could do."

It was the prostate cancer project and it was extremely important. He said, "What we need to do is to approach a better way of diagnosing so many clients when they come here. Every day we get 80 to 100 men that have been diagnosed with prostate cancer. Their diagnosis needs to be established by the end of the day because the next day we are due to get another 100."

So I set about doing the project by going over to the autopsy lab at Mayo Clinic and getting prostates from men who had died. I accumulated a couple every day and did a slicing procedure. And fortunately, one of my jobs during the summer (when I was going to college) was working in a meat market so I knew how to slice sausage. This wasn't much different but the prostate slices were thinner (3 mm each). I actually loaded them into little crates and took them down to histology. They made glass slides with the actual slice on it. Then I took high-speed, 35-millimeter pictures of those slides and used that as input into the computer memory. Once I got those slides into the memory, then it was a matter of organizing and registering the slides. They were every which way, so it was a difficult job to discover which one was first, second and so forth.

It was a weekend over the July 4th, or perhaps Memorial Day holiday. We were barbecuing chicken in back of the hotel where I was staying. I looked at those skewers in the end of the chicken as the chicken turned on the rotisserie and thought to myself, *"Well maybe I could develop a three-prong device in the form of a scalene triangle with equal sides. I could push it through the prostate before I slice it, with a little dye on the points."*

I was actually able to do it. Once the slicing, the crates, the histology and the photographing were done; then I put the slices with the three dots on it in the computer. I aligned them according to the dots of the scalene triangle. Once that was placed together, I could do the math on the projects, to find the area of the cancer. The urethra runs right through the prostate, so I was able to color that yellow or green, the prostate brown and the cancer was red. I would be able to calculate the surface area of the cancer or the volume of the cancer if it went down into the prostate like most often it does and provide a group of statistics for the actual prostate.

Once I had it perfected, then I had to do something different. After a lot of thinking and research, I visited the MRI, where they explained that the layers of MRI could serve the same way as my sliced layers. I adopted the MRI to actually achieve pictures of the pelvic area of men. Finally it was refined enough for me to separate out the prostate and then use the layering of the prostate to go into my program. It actually did the computation of the areas and volumes, and so forth. It was perfected after a two-year period (1991 to 1993).

Men coming to the Mayo Clinic would be given a card for a chest x-ray, a card for blood work, a card for urinalysis, and then also an MRI card. When they had an MRI of the pelvic area taken, it would be fed into my computer system, which did the rest of the work. So, at about 4:00 o'clock in the afternoon, Sterioff and Johnson and all the other surgeons would gather in a room and discuss these patients, and then would turn to the computer system that I had developed and actually review each patient individually with regard to how bad their condition was. The doctors could see how the patient's cancer of the prostate had progressed by checking out the numbers computed for surface areas, volumes and principal diagonals, and all the statistics and mathematics of it.

My program also generated a VCR movie of each patient's prostate showing top, bottom and all sides and angles. It could evaluate whether the patient needed a radical prostatectomy in the morning or two days from now, or if he needed radiation or hormonal treatment, or be sent home for a 90-day period and be asked to come back later for further evaluation.

This was my way of giving back, because they could run through all 80 or 100 men in the MRI and prostate cancer area there at Mayo Clinic and they would be able to determine a diagnosis for each man. That was in use for a few years; in fact, it's still in use in another version in a modified area to this date, I understand. It was a very rewarding thing to be able to give back.

I used that project for writing my PhD thesis because it was still something that was in my heart to do, from way back when the country schoolteacher had instilled in me a desire to finish educationally whatever I had started. It worked out well to write a thesis on prostate cancer, and I called it, "The Three-Dimensional Reconstruction of Prostate Cancer Using Image Processing."

It became a relatively thick book that I formulated for the University of Minnesota and Century University. My advisor for Minnesota was also a cancer patient and he was located in Albuquerque, New Mexico. He wanted me to do the thesis part of my degree through where he was affiliated at Century University; so, I did that. His name was Dr. Tom Burgess. He was grateful for what I had done in that area because it affected him a significant amount in his life. I was pleased that I could contribute in that way.

I finished all my requirements for my PhD in biostatistics in April of 1993 and went through the PhD degree graduation at Century University in May of that year. Most of my doctoral work had been completed in the early 1970's at the University of Minnesota; including all my PhD course work and all my PhD prelims (both oral and written). Dr. Tom Burgess had been my PhD advisor at Minnesota at that time. Then I had encountered many medical problems with regard to glaucoma surgeries and kidney dialysis and kidney transplants.

It was in my heart that God was directing me to complete my doctoral degree to finalize my formal education that Mrs. Steiner had started back in Cudd School many years earlier. Hence, I was able to write my PhD thesis and at the same time, help a lot of men in doing it. I was glad that Dr. Tom Burgess was still available to see me through to completion of my Doctoral Degree, and to benefit him health wise also. Praise God! Thank you Jesus!

In the fall terms of 1993 and 1994, I taught mathematics and statistics at the University of Wisconsin-River Falls and then returned to Tucson, Arizona for the winter season. Dr. Sterioff had recommended for me to tutor math and statistics for the University Of Arizona Math Department for those two winter seasons.

18. ROSE

It was during fall of 1993 that I realized I had been on my own for a long enough time, since the divorce in 1989. I yearned to find a good Christian lady to be my next wife. I had put a distance between the drunken woman (who was nothing but trouble) and myself. I was now looking for a good woman to be equally yoked with. Having God in my life, I thought the best place to look was at church, either Eastside Assembly of God or the River Falls Assembly of God. My blindness (legal) did not permit me to do very well at this.

I joined a singles club called 'Singles Direct Call' in Tucson and was interviewed by a lady of the organization. After a couple of hours, she concluded that I'd need a very special lady. I had a couple of dates with women from the club, but found no one I was interested in.

I decided to make a list of what I wanted in a Christian lady and then to pray about it. My list was not one like most men would construct, but it was what I felt I needed in a new relationship with a lady. My list is as follows:

1. A person who would like to read to me from the Bible, newspaper, etc.

2. Someone to drive a car (I had cars but no driver).

3. A kind, helpful, considerate, and loving person.

4. Blond hair and blue eyes.

5. Physically attractive, less than 135 lbs., 5'8" or 5'9" tall.

6.   Born again and spirit filled.

7.   A good cook and enjoyed eating out.

8.   Liked to walk, dance, play cards, travel, and do almost everything together.

9.   Was a very happy, joyful, and positive person.

I put this list by my bed on the night table and proceeded to pray about it, asking God to bring me such a Christian lady. I prayed each night on my knees by my bed before retiring, and believed that God would find the right woman for me. On the 180th day of prayer, about 4 p.m. in the afternoon, my telephone rang. I answered it and there was a kind-sounding lady who was calling. Her name was Rosemary Jordan! I asked if she was a Christian lady and she said that she was a born again and spirit-filled Christian! By this time, I had everything on the list in my memory so I asked Rosemary about all 9 points on my list. She answered everything in correct order. I knew that God had sent me potentially my new wife! Thank you Jesus!

I explained my challenges with vision and hearing and she said they are "no problem". She said she would be happy to be the driver of our car and would help me in everything she could. We talked a little more on the telephone and I asked if she would like to go out to dinner in the next few days. She said, "Yes." I asked her to pick me up at my office at the University Of Arizona statistics department on the evening of March 1, 1994. She agreed.

On March 1 at 6 p.m., there was a rap on my office door and when I opened it, there stood a beautiful blond lady with blue eyes who was physically attractive, slender, and about 5'8" tall. My first thought as I looked at her was, "Oh dear God, You've sent me an angel."

She was pretty and glamorous and had everything I had asked God for on my list. Praise God! I asked her to come in and sit down and we proceeded to talk and to get to know each other. She said I could call her Rose if I desired. We talked a little more and then decided we should go and dine. Rose was exceptionally kind and loving in her nature, and we hit it off immediately.

Rose drove, and we went to the Blue Willow Restaurant on Campbell Avenue in Tucson and enjoyed a very nice dinner on the patio of the

Blue Willow. We had great conversation at dinner and she told me about herself and that her husband had died of a rare kidney disease several years ago. She revealed to me about her varied background in business as a manager of a couple of entities and now she was taking care of children in her home over on Tuttle Avenue in Tucson. She had been in Tucson since 1980, having moved from Riverside, California. I told her about myself also. We were instantly close friends and it seemed like we had known each other for many, many years.

After dinner and much conversation, we left the restaurant and Rose drove me to my condo off 22nd Street in Tucson. We went to my place and talked for another couple of hours. I asked her how she knew to call me and she told me that she had belonged to "Singles Direct Call." Rose explained that the club had sent her several lists of available men. She had asked two of the mothers of children she had cared for to look at the lists and help her decide whom to call. They all decided on my ad that had been constructed more than two years ago, the one I had forgotten about. My ad said something about being a college professor and a Christian, so they all decided that Rose should call me on my 180th day of prayer (unknown to them). I believe that God was answering my prayer and had made these arrangements with the help of three Christian ladies who all made the same selection on a document of available men. Thank you Jesus!

There was a bowl of Valentine hearts on the coffee table in my living room in a dish, and later in our conversation Rose handed me a heart and it said, "May I kiss you!"

I said "certainly" and we kissed and kissed and hugged and hugged for about an hour or so. We seemed to fall in love that evening; yes, we did. I later walked Rose to her car. We kissed and hugged some more. Neither of us wanted to say good night. Finally, she asked if she could come pick me up again tomorrow evening and take me to her house. She would make me dinner at 7 p.m. I accepted, and believe me it was hard to let her go. I finally accepted the situation and returned to my condo, higher than a kite. I knew that God had answered my prayer and I was incredibly, exceptionally happy!

The next evening Rose came by my office at the U of A about 5:30 p.m. and after a warm greeting she drove me over to her home on Tuttle Avenue in West Tucson. Rose had a nice 3 bedroom, 2 bath home with

2 extra rooms that were filled with cribs, mattresses, toys, and other children's items. Her home was very comfortable and it had several fruit trees in the back yard. It was pleasant to see three wonderful large trees loaded with grapefruit, lemons and oranges respectively. Having been from the Midwest, I was not used to seeing these fruit trees. It was a real joy to be with Rose at her home.

We enjoyed an excellent dinner that evening and I realized that she *was* a good cook. We prayed before we ate and had wonderful conversation throughout the evening. I felt we were yoked together in our spirits because we both loved the Lord! It was like we knew each other for a long time even though we had met just yesterday. At the close of the evening, Rose drove me home to my condo. We kissed and hugged and made plans to attend her church on Sunday morning and my church Sunday evening. We were alike and close in so many ways that it was hard to part and go to separate houses.

Rosemary was a little older but that did not seem to make a difference to either of us. It reminded me that I had not specified any age on my list of 9 items that I had prayed on for 180 days. I counseled myself that God wants us to pray specifically for our requests. In this case it did not make a difference because of all the other similarities.

In Tucson I enjoy using Van Tran Service, which is a transportation service for challenged people. I made a reservation with Van Tran to go to Saint James Methodist Church on Sunday morning on Campbell Avenue. I met Rosie there and we went to Sunday school where she introduced me to all her friends; I enjoyed meeting each one of them. We then attended the worship service at Saint James Methodist where we prayed, sang together and listened to Pastor Gary Roper preach. I enjoyed the service and really took pleasure that Rosie and I could worship the Lord together.

Back in Wisconsin, I had been raised in the Lutheran church from early childhood so the Methodist church was quite similar. After I had been born again and spirit filled in 1982, I had become a DFL (defrosted Lutheran) and attended a much more lively service at the Assembly of God on Wilmot Avenue in Tucson for my spiritual nourishment. Bob and Joan had taken me to such a church the next day after being born again. There is nothing wrong with the traditional churches such as Lutheran, Methodist, or Catholic — but after being born again and having Jesus in my heart I needed to worship where they "do something" like prayer, healing, deliverance, and salvation during the service rather than just talking about it such as, "We'll pray for you this week (if we remember)." The Assembly of God Church is a do-something church. If someone needs healing, the Assembly Church will have a healing line right then during the service and pray for whoever needs healing. Praise God! The Eastside Assembly of God (ESAG) is a Bible-believing church where every sermon is preached right from God's word! Once you are born again and spirit filled, you are "on fire for Jesus" and you want to worship with other born again Christians!

That Sunday evening at 7 p.m., I took her to her first Assembly of God service at Eastside Assembly Of God Church at 1930 S. Wilmot Road, to hear Pastor David L. Stevens, a fantastic, wonderful preacher of God's word! Rosie enjoyed the service and said she felt at home there and would like to worship at the Assembly from then on when we were together. When she listened to Pastor Stevens' sermon that first night she fell in great favor for his preaching God's word. Pastor Stevens was a former Marine in the Vietnam War and he preached with a lot of fire, compassion, and gusto! She loved it! I remember the first time I heard Pastor Stevens preach; I thought the Bible was jumping out at me. My instant desire was to serve, witness, and win disciples for the Lord! I wanted to be in God's army and I joined immediately! Thank you Jesus!

Rosie and I worshipped at Eastside from that point on and she invited her Sunday school class at St. James to come hear Pastor Stevens at Eastside and they came the next Sunday! Thank you Jesus!

Rosie and I continued to see each other almost every day. Our relationship became deeper and our love grew richer for each other. Rosie's kind, patient, and loving manner transferred to me, and we were one in the spirit on all occasions. We enjoyed baseball games, dancing, and jazz music and definitely took pleasure in worshipping the Lord together.

At the end of April 1994, we decided to get married and live as one in the Lord! After a nice dinner on a Saturday night, I asked Rosie if she would marry me. She said "yes" and was so excited that she could hardly stand still. I told her that we certainly loved each other so we should share our lives together in marriage, as the Lord directs. I also gave her a very nice diamond ring that evening. We were both so happy and excited that we could hardly sleep! The next day, Sunday, we worshipped the Lord and told all our friends the good news. Praise God!

That Sunday afternoon and during the next week we made plans for our wedding day. We decided on June 25, 1994 to be our wedding date. We both were ecstatic and so excited that we could hardly stand still. We made plans that my son would be my best man and Rosie's daughter, Debbie, would be her matron of honor. Mark would come from Minnesota and Debbie would come from California to Tucson, Arizona. We decided to have some of Rosie's daycare kids be in the wedding too. So Jessica (9) and Angie (11) were bridesmaids. They both had been under Rosie's care since their births. Also the little flower girl, Laura (6) and little red-haired Scottie (4) was the ring bearer. Those two kids looked so cute together.

My brother Ron was an usher and a close GA friend Roger was the other usher who lit the candles on the altar. Due to the fact that we both had been married before, Pastor Stevens said we would have to be married in Rose's church which was St. James Methodist on Campbell Ave. Pastor Stevens blessed us both and said he would have Pastor Bill Seal from ESAG take part in the wedding at St James. So Pastor Gary Roper from St James and Pastor Seal from ESAG made plans together to do our wedding.

Almost two months later on June 25, 1994, the wedding between Rosemary Jordan and Lyndon C. Weberg took place at St James Church at 2 p.m. It was a beautiful summer day in Tucson, Arizona. The midday temperature hit 117 degrees; it was hot! It was cool in the church but an extremely hot, dry summer day outside. The temp had not been anywhere close to 117 for more than 15 years of living in Tucson, but that day was one hot day!

The wedding went very smoothly with everyone doing his or her part during the service. The church was crowded with friends, neighbors, GA people, parents of the children that Rose had taken care of, and ESAG people. It was a very warm, joyous group. Rosie was stunning; so beautiful. She was lovely, in a light pink dress with a striking rose-colored hat.

I was elated that we were getting married. Thank you Jesus! All the men were dressed in black tuxedos and everyone looked sharp! Little

Scottie, the ring bearer was a little darling with his date Laura for the day. Their parents were excited for their children in Rosie's wedding. Everyone was happy for her, and for the both of us.

Pastor Roper did the main officiating of the wedding and gave a nice talk about Rose and Lyn. Pastor Seal sang "The Lord's Prayer" magnificently. He also gave the blessing for the ring ceremony. It all worked out great!

Pastor Seal was the pastor at ESAG who had given the sermon on a Wednesday evening about "mountain top experience" that had helped me to get over grieving for my daughter, Stephanie. I'm still blessed to this day, for the help I received that Wednesday evening. Thank you Jesus!

Following the wedding, there were a multitude of hugs and kisses outside the church. Then we all went to the Marriott Hotel in Tucson for the wedding reception. We had a wonderful time eating, drinking and being merry, visiting, laughing, and joking about the past. We all enjoyed ourselves for several hours into the evening. Finally the guests, friends, relatives and wedding goers went to their homes, and Rosie and I went to the wedding suite at the Marriott for our first night as newlyweds.

The next afternoon we spent time with my son Mark, my brother Ron, and Rosie's daughter before we left them to go on our honeymoon to the White Mountains in northern Arizona. About a week after our honeymoon, we returned to Tucson and began our lives together as a loving married couple together. At this writing, Rosie and I are still on our honeymoon, over 15 years later. We're living as one in the Lord and still hug and kiss many times a day. The Lord has truly blessed us in every way. Even today we say "I love you" when just passing one another in our large house, or if we're going to be apart for a short time from each other. When others ask us how we are doing, we often say, "We're still on our honeymoon!"

We sold Rosie's house on the west side of Tucson, and lived in co-ops and condos for the next 10 years. Then in 2004, we bought a beautiful Santa Fe style home in central Tucson. This home is convenient to many attractions in the main part of Tucson. And it is our home together where we reside and enjoy the beautiful Southwest. I have continued to teach University and to do research in cancer and Alzheimer's disease at the University of Arizona. Rosie has been busy as a caregiver to seniors and in real estate.

I often think about my list that I prayed for when I was looking for a wife. Point 1 was that I needed someone to read to me being I'm legally blind. This request showed me how God often doubly and triply blesses you when you make a supplication.

In this case, Rosie is an avid reader and reads book after book. She reads the Sunday paper from the front page to the ads in the back. She will stop whatever she is doing to read something to me with a very willing spirit to help, even after 15 years or more. I have CC-TVs and JAWS on my computer, which reads out loud 99% of what I need to read, but Rosie is so special; she's willing to stop and read anything to me.

This showed me how God blessed me with this request. He blessed me also with all the prayer requests that I prayed for faithfully for 180 days. Every day, when I see Rosie cut up the vegetables and fruit into hundreds of pieces, I know that God has blessed me richly with an excellent cook and fantastic dinner preparer. Praise God!

I should mention that any married couple will have a "few moments of intense fellowship" on occasion. Rosie and I learned that if this should occur, we talk it out immediately. We forgive one another and give each other a hug and kiss, and go on our merry way. We have had very few of these situations but each one has been resolved in less than 5 minutes, and then we continue our loving life together. Thank you Jesus!

19. MINISTRIES

Rosie and I worship the Lord every day with Bible reading and much prayer together, and on our own. We attend Eastside Assembly of God twice on Sundays and once on Wednesday evening to receive spiritual nourishment and to praise God and thank Him for all his blessings! We both stay on fire for Jesus in our everyday lives. Due to "wanting to serve the Lord" we are involved in several ministries. These are as follows:

1.   Prison fellowship (27 years-Lyn; 15 years-Rosie)

2.   Homeless ministry (2 years-Lyn)

3.   Alcoholics Anonymous (AA) ministry for Jesus (27 years-Lyn)

4.   Gamblers Anonymous (GA) ministry for Jesus (27 years-Lyn)

5.   Missionettes (girls)(15 years-Rosie)

6.   Sanctuary Choir (10 years-Rosie)

7.   Templo Betel Spanish Church (1 year-Lyn)

Plus many other daily ways of witnessing for Jesus!

For about 26-27 years, ever since I was born again and spirit filled on 10/19/82, I have had a Smile Book ministry. These little books with a big round yellow smile face on them say, "smile!" on top of the face, and say, "Jesus loves you!" on the bottom. They are about 3 in. by 2 in. in size and have about 10 pages of Bible verses and what to do to become a Christian.

I've found it very easy to hand them to people and ask "May I give you a smile book today?" When they take one I usually ask immediately, "Do you know Jesus, do you have a personal relationship with Jesus?" Then the conversation begins and I can witness Jesus to them or thank them for being a follower of the Lord already! These little books have won many, many people to Jesus, or have watered the person's spirit enough so the next individual witnessing Jesus may be the one to lead someone to the Lord! I've ordered these books 5,000 at a time from "Sowers of the Seed" Ministry in Houston, Texas.

I keep a stack of the little books by the door that I most frequently use, and before I leave the house I reach down and take a big handful of Smile Books. I jam them into a pocket where they can be easily reached. Then I give a Smile Book to whomever I encounter in the day – Van Tran drivers, clerks, waitresses, doctors, dentists, AA and GA people, dialysis people, and on and on – who ever God puts in my path that day, and every day. My brief case is loaded with Smile Books. They go to prison, homeless ministry and church, to sporting events, and so on and so forth. I also have Spanish Smile Books for Spanish ministry.

There are many examples of people accepting Jesus. One is about Monica, who Rosie and I met for the first time on 6/6/06 in the Arizona Shuttle at the Phoenix airport at about 6:30 a.m. when we were returning from vacation. The three of us boarded the shuttle going from Phoenix to Tucson, and Monica sat in front of us. After we had been on the road for about 5 minutes, I reached over the back of the seat between us and asked her, "May I give you a Smile Book this morning?"

Her reply to me was, "How did you know that I was so sad today?"

I said, "I didn't know you were sad, I was just giving this little book to be friendly and to find out if you knew Jesus."

She said, "My name is Monica"

I told her, "My name is Lyn and this is my wife, Rose. Why are you so sad today?"

Monica said, "I'm sad because my husband has just run off with another woman, and I'm going back to Tucson to be with my mom and my two younger children."

I continued to talk to Monica as we traveled, and finally got around to asking her, "Do you have a personal relationship with Jesus Christ?"

She explained that she had been brought up Catholic and there was nothing ever said about having a personal relationship with Jesus Christ, in the Catholic Church. It was all about the priest, the pope, and a bunch of undistinguishable Latin that no one could understand. I then gave her my testimony of how Jesus Christ came into my life, and that both Rose and I had been saved! I explained that 'saved' meant if we were killed in an accident tonight that we were saved and would go to heaven! I told Monica what it meant to be born again and spirit-filled and she could gain this status by saying the Sinner's Prayer and accepting Jesus into her heart! I told her about Eastside Assembly of God and invited her to attend that evening, since it was Sunday.

She thought for a moment and then said, "Yes, yes, I do want to go tonight!" Thank you Holy Spirit!

We were nearing Tucson, so I asked her if we could pick her up later to go to ESAG. She said she would meet us there at 7 p.m. I gave her the directions and she assured us that she would be there. She even gave us her telephone number. Monica was excited and I knew in my heart that she would be there.

That Sunday evening we met Monica and her two children, Christina (10) and Richard (13). We all sat in the first or second row forward so I could see. They liked the service with its joyous songs praising and thanking God for all his blessings. There was much prayer and a healing line for people needing physical healing. Then a great sermon, full of fire and gusto, straight from God's word, The Holy Bible! We all listened intently to the sermon and were excited about its contents and meaning for our lives. When the sermon time had ended, Pastor Kraft gave the invitation for people to accept Jesus. He asked them to come forward for prayer and to say the Sinner's Prayer and gain a personal relationship with Jesus.

After the altar call had started and there were people heading toward the front, Monica, Christina and Richard all got up at the same time and went forward to accept Jesus! Rosie and I stood behind them with our arms raised, praising and thanking God. I know that the angels in heaven were dancing and worshipping God for the new souls that were brought into the kingdom that glorious evening!

We gave them hugs and welcomed them into the family of God! Many other people in the church greeted and congratulated them. Monica said, "I really feel at home here, and it's a 'do something church'. If you need prayer, they do it right then and there for you. There's no waiting!"

All three of them said, "I feel Jesus in my heart! I feel happy and joyous even though I have these earthly problems."

We all went to dinner, and afterwards Rosie and I gave Monica and her children a Bible and instructed them to begin reading in the book of John in the New Testament. We explained that daily reading of the Bible is necessary to continue a personal relationship with Jesus!

We talked on the telephone Monday and Tuesday and invited them to return to ESAG on Wednesday for another uplifting service. I told Monica that you need to get nourished spiritually at least twice a week and read the Bible and pray in between to stay healthy spiritually. Just as we need food for our physical nourishment, we also need food for spiritual nourishment, and to experience being close to God. This kind of balance leads to a happy and joyous life in the Lord!

I told her if you get down or depressed at times, simply say "the joy of the Lord is my strength!" and this will lift you right up again. Think about this, that you are saved and no matter what happens, you are going to heaven! In about a month, after giving their lives to Jesus, Monica, Richard and Christina were all baptized in water by immersion at ESAG, which is the first act of obedience to the Lord! All born again, spirit filled Christians are baptized in water shortly after they are born again.

Rosie and I have continued to assist Monica in her walk with the Lord, as well as ESAG helping her in many ways. We will continue to support her in any way that we can. She and her children are our witnesses.

A second example of a Smile Book promoting a soul salvation is as follows: This was back in River Falls, WI about 20 some years ago. I was down on a semi-busy street on a Saturday morning passing out Smile

Books to whoever came by. For bikers, I just hold them up and they take it as the bike goes by. After a few hours of passing out these books on the street and talking with some people, I returned home for the rest of the day. It was one of the fall terms that I was teaching at UW-RF.

The following Thursday evening, I was scheduled to speak at the local Kinnic Falls Halfway House where I once attended to help find sobriety. On that particular night, I was scheduled to give my story of recovery. Rosie sang a Christian song and when I was through speaking, a stocky man with black hair named Bob came to me and said, "You don't remember, but last Saturday you gave me one of those Smile Books. It says, 'Smile! Jesus loves you!' Will you tell me more? I'm a Jew and do not know what this means."

Rosie and I said we would be happy to explain. We went for coffee and began to explain the story of how Jesus is the Way of salvation. We agreed to get together next at the South Fork restaurant in River Falls. A few days later we met Bob and further explained about the Lord. This tutorial continued with Bob. We got to know him better and discovered he was from Los Angeles. Rosie had been from California so the two of them had much to talk over. Two weeks later, Delores who was the assistant director at the Kinnic Falls Halfway House called me at my UW-RF office and asked, "Lyn, are you planning to go to Arizona again this winter?"

I said, "Yes, I'm planning on that."

"Can I send a man over to see you about leasing your condo when you are away?"

I told Delores that would be fine. At the designated time there was a rap at the door and when I opened it, there stood Bob, the same Bob who we were witnessing to on a regular basis.

I greeted him and we sat and talked awhile. Bob told me he was getting out of the halfway house about the time we were planning to leave for Tucson, Arizona. He gave me his story and said he had to stay in the River Falls area for 7 years for his sobriety before he could return to his home in Los Angeles because of his relapse history. Delores assured me Bob was really serious about his sobriety and that he had money and that he would take care of my place.

We drew a short lease agreement and he had a place to live until the summer of the next year. We continued to witness and minister to Bob and took him to the River Falls Assembly Of God church on several occasions. Before we left for Arizona, Bob said the Serenity Prayer and invited Jesus into his heart. He started reading the Bible and began to pray many times a day. Rosie and I have become good friends with Bob and after he spent 7 years in Wisconsin he returned to his home in Los Angeles. We stay in contact with him. Bob loves horses so he has come to Tucson on several occasions to look at small ranches that he might like to purchase. He always attends church with us at ESAG. He has become good friends with Jim and Phyllis Brown, and we've all been out to Jim's small ranch where he has two horses.

As a result of a Smile Book given to a biker one Saturday morning, Bob knows and has a personal relationship with Jesus Christ. He knows that spiritual nourishment is necessary to remain spiritually fed, and because of that his life of sobriety goes smoothly one day at a time. This little book has given Lyn and Rose a wonderful friend in Bob that we still enjoy almost 30 years later.

A third story about the Smile Book at work occurred with a man named John from Ethiopia. I had 40 acres of vacant land for sale at Casa Grande, Arizona. A man named John called me from California. He called me in Tucson and asked if he could come over and look at this property. We arranged a time and place and Rose and I drove to Casa Grande on Saturday morning to pick up John at his hotel room. When he got into the back, I handed John a Smile Book and Rose and I heard a loud voice come from the back seat.

John said in a loud, exuberant voice, "Boy! Do I know Jesus! I am so glad that I know Jesus! I am so glad that America sent missionaries to my country Ethiopia when I was only 6 years old! I got to go to Sunday School and to Vacation Bible School for many years as a child growing up! I am so glad that I know Jesus and that I am saved! I am going to heaven and I am so happy!"

He went on for 20-30 minutes about how thankful he was that the Christian church sent missionaries to his country, Ethiopia! We all were so excited about John's testimony that nothing else mattered, including the land. When we arrived at the property we all got out of the car and walked on the land. John walked for about 10 minutes on the land and he said, "I want to buy this land!" We went to a restaurant and wrote up the contract for the nice 40 acres.

This started a long and lasting friendship with John and we continue to witness to John and he continues to witness to us. What a Christian brother! I send him tapes from ESAG and he calls me and goes through the same excited testimony as before. This is the most positive response I have gotten so far in passing out Smile Books! God is so good!

A duplicate of a Smile Book that I have been passing out for the past 27 years with many stories of salvation for the Lord Jesus is as follows:

Lyndon Weberg

DO YOU
EVER FEEL
LIKE NOBODY
REALLY CARES?

The Bible says, "**For all have sinned and come short of the glory of God.**" Romans chapter 3, verse 23.

Have you ever lied or taken anything that belonged to someone else? Then you have sinned, haven't you?

If we die in our sins, we are eternally lost and forever separated from God. But God offers another way. If we are willing to turn from our sins, we can have eternal life free as a gift. This means we can't earn it by being good, or

Suppose you had an incurable disease, and one day you read of a doctor who had discovered the cure for that disease. Let's suppose he offered to give you this cure free.

HAVE YOU TAKEN THE STEP OF FAITH TO RECEIVE JESUS CHRIST PERSONALLY, AS YOUR SAVIOUR?

If your best friend
knocked at the door
of your house, what
would you say to him?

**YOU WOULD SAY
"COME IN,"
WOULDN'T YOU?**

WHAT WILL YOUR ANSWER BE?

You can receive Jesus right now if this prayer expresses the desire of your heart:

Which
Choice Did
You Make

WHO IS A CHRISTIAN?

You are a Christian
if your choice was to
turn from your sins
and personally invite
Jesus Christ to become
Lord of your life.

How do you know?

Jesus said, "I **WILL** come in."

Revelation chapter 3, verse 20.

1st letter of John, chapter 5, verses 11—13.

For God took the sinless Christ and laid on Him our sins. Then, in exchange, He gives God's goodness to us!

Continue reading your Bible. It's truths are true today and forever.

For Extra Copies Write: SOWERS OF SEED, INC. P. O. BOX 6217 FT. WORTH, TX. 76115 U.S.A. www.sowersofseed.com 1-800-923-6304 "Brethren, pray for us.

20. MONEY MATTERS

"The love of money is the root of all evil!" from I Timothy 6:10, described me for the first 38 years of my life. Money was my god! This was especially true during my gambling years of 1969 to 1982. As the gambling progressed, money became less of a focus because the action of gambling completely took over. I had to be in 'action' every minute of the day and night. The money was negligible and simply was the means of getting the 'action' and proved to almost be my total downfall, but thank God, I found Gamblers Anonymous and shortly thereafter I found Jesus! The 'pressure relief group' of Gamblers Anonymous was especially instrumental in removing money as a god in my life.

About 30 days clean in GA my sponsor took me to pressure relief for financial, legal, and marital problems in my life. In the GA pressure relief meeting, my wife and I brought all our bills and income sources to the meeting and the pressure group worked out a budget to pay all our bills and to pay my bookies on a monthly basis. Members of the pressure relief group handled all the credit card bills and the bookies. I am thankful to this day that Jim C and Stafford K were able to work out monthly payments with these creditors. Jim C. even was able to get the credit cards to forgo the interest and to reduce the principal somewhat. Stafford was able to cut a deal with the bookies. A bookie from Eau Claire, WI told him he now had 18 ex-gamblers paying him on a monthly basis. He said that this income augmented his retirement income, so he was willing to add another.

The most important thing for me in the pressure relief group was that I was put on an allowance of $25 a week (1982). I was so ashamed of this small amount that I broke down and cried. I had been a highflying stockbroker for three years and was used to making $2,000 to $5,000 per day, and now "$25 a week?" I screamed, "How can I live on this drop in the bucket?"

My sponsor Stafford K. said, "You do not have to worry about any other money issues because your budget will pay all your expenses. The $25 is yours to spend on you, so be good to yourself and buy a strawberry sundae at the Dairy Queen for not gambling today. You can buy yourself a new pair of shoestrings for your shoes."

Stafford was right. The pressure relief group took away my obsession with money, as I had been doing for years up to this point. It was a big relief not to have money on my mind all the time. My wife and I wrote out the bills together so I felt I had a part in paying the bills too. My wife, Jean, was a GAM A NON member and that group suggested that we pay the bills together.

I learned to like the allowance over the next two years of recovery. It allowed me to find other things to do, rather than gamble and think about money all of the time. I even learned to save money on my allowance. I remember how good it felt when I had saved $400 and I could put it into a savings account. I learned to like the peace of mind because it gave me complete freedom from all the other money concerns. We reviewed the budget and my allowance and the pressure relief group made slight adjustments in our budget from time to time. The pressure relief group was especially pleased when they learned that I had been saving my allowance and had opened a savings account. To this day, some 27 years later, I am thankful for the GA Pressure Relief Group and my GAM A NON wife Jean, who helped immensely. I am thankful to Jean who had the stamina and strength to hang in there during the time of early recovery for both of us. Thank God! Thank God for GA AND GAM A NON, and their programs to help people and families who have been affected by compulsive gambling. They helped me in my struggles to take the love of money out of my life and mind.

With my being born again and spirit filled and back into God's Kingdom, I also learned that money was to be used to pay bills and to go out for dinner or to a movie once a week. The GA budget also had an amount for dinner or a movie on a weekly basis too. I have learned that I am a steward of the money God gives us to live on from period to period. Between the GA program and my Christian faith, I have a completely different and useful idea about money. It is far different than it used to be in my old life.

Malachi 3:19 says: "Bring all the tithes into the storehouse so all will be full and I promise to open the windows of heavens and to pour out blessings 30, 60 and 100 fold so large so that your bags will be running over and overflowing so many blessings that you cannot contain them."

The tithe is 10% of your increase; this should be given to the Lord! The first fruits, or the best, should be given to the Lord and not your leftovers. This type of giving is a way of worshipping the Lord and I've found from experience that God does open the windows of heaven and pours out His blessings 30, 60 and 100 fold. I suggest that you try this too, and watch the Lord keep his promise. God says, "Try Me and see that I will prove my word correct." Tithing is a great principle and I can assure you that I have been doubly blessed and more!

When a person stops gambling (or any other addiction), one feels empty and without any thing to do to make life seem realistic or joyful. The preoccupation of the gambling ran my life for many years. I was totally preoccupied with thinking about money. Where am I going to get money for the next bet, or to pay the bookies? When I stopped gambling I needed a new preoccupation and I am ever thankful to Barb Wall, my piano teacher. I started to play the piano to help forget about gambling. Since I am legally blind, Barb and her daughter made me oversized pages of music with very large notes on them so I could learn to read music. The whole note was the size of a quarter or larger. I had to concentrate so hard on seeing those music notes that it helped me get over the preoccupation of the addiction. I am thankful to Barb and her daughter for helping me with my early recovery.

Luke 16:13 and Matthew 6:24 say, *"You cannot serve God and money at the same time. You will either love one or hate the other."* I learned during my early recovery and until today to love God first, and all the other blessings come later.

21. SATAN

I must include a small amount about Satan in this book too. Many years ago, one of the angels in heaven became very arrogant and prideful. He wanted to be God. His name was Lucifer. God eventually ousted Lucifer from heaven and about a third of the angels went with him. His new name was Satan.

That is still the situation. God is in heaven with two thirds of His angels and Satan and one third of his angels are down here on earth. Satan's mission in this world is to kill, steal, and destroy! There is a constant spiritual battle going on in the heavenlies and the battle is over souls (your mind, emotions, and will). God wants souls to spend eternity in heaven with Him, while Satan wants souls to spend eternity in hell. Heaven is a very nice and wonderful place while hell is a terrible place of fires, misery, and gnashing of teeth forever and ever.

This is why each person needs to decide where they want to spend eternity (eternity is forever and ever and ever and ever...) Do you want to stay for eternity in a beautiful mansion that God has prepared for you, or do you want to spend forever and ever in a burning pit of fire with Satan whipping you at every opportunity?

I choose God! I know the outcome of the battle. I know that God wins! For an ex-gambler, I'm in a WIN –WIN situation! Praise God! Praise God!

I Peter 5:8 says, *"Be sober and vigilant, the devil stalks around like a roaring lion seeking who he may devour!"* James 4:7 reveals, *"Resist the devil and he will flee!"*

We must use these verses to ward off the devil when he comes. For example, if you are tempted to steal something in a store or to commit adultery with a woman, you must speak to the devil and say, "In the name of Jesus Christ, I say to you devil, 'Get out of here!'" At the name of Jesus, the devil runs and does not come back. The devil knows that he was defeated at the Cross by Jesus!

If you have disbelief and need to see the work of the devil, turn the evening news on your TV and you'll see firsthand the destruction, death, rape and his mission to kill, steal and destroy! Resist the devil and he will flee! When you have accomplished this, then you'll be able to help more people in resisting the devil! God will bless you!

22. DRAW NEAR TO GOD EVERY DAY!

James 4:8 says, "Draw near to God and God will draw near to you." Every day I must draw near to God so God will draw near to me. This is a 'must' in this world, if you want to keep God in your life. I know that I must make the effort each day. So I pray before I get out of bed, read the Bible, read the Upper Room devotion book and pray in the closet where I have my alone time with God on a daily basis. Then I pray continuously throughout the day. My wife and I attend church several times a week and serve at the church, in order to draw near to God. The first Tuesday of each month, we go to church (ESAG) and pray for an hour straight for our country, city, missionaries, family, and on and on. Prayer works; and God gives answers when we need them. Please read the 5 chapters of the book of James soon. It will get you going in the right direction. This is why I minister daily to others because God's will is that no one should perish.

Satan will be thrown into the burning lake of sulfur during the White Throne Judgment. This is why we must serve God in the mission of saving of souls every day. For it is God's will that no one should perish, but all should come to repentance. So please work with me on saving souls!

In conclusion, I have written this book so it would be a witness for Jesus, a testimony of my life, and an encouragement to all the readers to accept Jesus as their Savior. I have indicated how I found the Lord after a life of destruction and despair, so no matter what your situation might be – I want to encourage you to find Jesus so your life might be changed just as mine was. No situation is too difficult for God to change for the better. After all we are all God's children. He has created each of us and has a particular purpose for our individual lives.

We are placed for a short time here on earth. Everything in this world becomes worse as time goes by in regard to the breaking of God's will through abortion, same sex marriages, murders, stealing, etc. Satan is the prince of this world and his mission is to kill, steal, and destroy. The only hope we have as God's people is to cling to the Lord Jesus as our salvation. If we do this we will become winners at last!

I say frequently, "We have nothing in this world to hang on to that gives us any assurance so the only thing that is solid ground is Jesus Christ! We also know this is right because the last chapter in the Bible says, "We win!" So we wait for the Rapture to come and take us home to Jesus!

If you are unsure of your future, please say this sinner's prayer and come to the Lord: Dear Jesus, I_____, ask You, Jesus, to come into my heart today. I accept You as my Savior. Please forgive every sin that I have committed and remove all of them from me as far as the east is from the west. Put Your love in my heart and let me serve and witness for You all the rest of my earthly life. Thank You Jesus, for saving my soul! Today I will serve You, and continue to all the rest of my earthly days!

If you have said the prayer and really meant it, your name has just been written in the Book of Life. You have been saved! The angels in heaven are rejoicing for you because you have just come into the Kingdom of God! You need to believe the words of this prayer and your decision, and always remember the date you were saved. My salvation date is 10/19/82. That is the date my name was written down in the Book of Life. I am very happy about this every day of my life; I praise and thank God for this miracle. The Book of Life will be opened at the White Throne Judgment and if your name is written there you will go to heaven, that glorious place that God has prepared for us forever and ever!

If your name is not found in the Book of Life at the time of the White Throne Judgment, you will be thrown into the lake of fire and sulfur, to be with Satan and all his followers. You will go down to hell forever and ever with total separation from God. There will be complete darkness in the abyss and you will hear the gnashing of teeth as Satan's followers are punished and beaten unmercifully!!

You have nothing to lose and everything to gain by asking Jesus into your heart to live. After you accept Jesus, you must strengthen your personal relationship with Him on a daily basis by reading God's Word (the Bible) every day, praying (talking to God) daily, going to a full gospel church to have fellowship with the followers of the Lord, and serving Him by helping others become closer to Him.

If you do this you are ready for the Rapture, which is coming any day now! The time is short, so witness for the Lord to your family, fellow workers, friends, and strangers! The Lord Jesus is coming soon. Praise God! Praise God! Thank You Jesus!

Oh, that I might be a greeter at heaven's door and be responsible for shining the door knobs on the many mansions that the Lord Jesus has set up for us to live forever and ever! Amen.

Some Bible Stories and Bible verses will follow to support this book. These are just a few from God's Bible. Secure a Christian Bible and read and read!

23. INSPIRATIONAL SECTION OF CHRISTIAN HYMNS, BIBLE STORIES, AND BIBLE VERSES

Christian Hymns

How Great Thou Art - *Stuart Hine*

Then sings my soul my Savior God to Thee
How great Thou art How great Thou art
Then sings my soul my Savior God to Thee
How great Thou art How great Thou art

Verse 1
O Lord my God when I in awesome wonder
Consider all the worlds Thy hands have made
I see the stars I hear the rolling thunder
Thy pow'r thru'out the universe displayed

Verse 2
When thru the woods and forest glades I wander
And hear the birds sing sweetly in the trees
When I look down from lofty mountain grandeur
And hear the brook and feel the gentle breeze

Verse 3
And when I think that God His Son not sparing
Sent Him to die I scarce can take it in
That on the cross my burden gladly bearing
He bled and died to take away my sin

Verse 4
When Christ shall come with shout of acclamation
And take me home what joy shall fill my heart
Then I shall bow in humble adoration
And there proclaim my God how great Thou art

Amazing Grace - *John Newton*

Verse 1

Amazing grace how sweet the sound
That saved a wretch like me
I once was lost but now am found
Was blind but now I see

Verse 2

'Twas grace that taught my heart to fear
And grace my fears relieved
How precious did that grace appear
The hour I first believed

Verse 3

Through many dangers toils and snares
I have already come
'Tis grace has brought me safe thus far
And grace will lead me home

Verse 4

When we've been there ten thousand years
Bright shining as the sun
We've no less days to sing God's praise
Than when we've first begun

It Is Well With My Soul - *Horatio Spafford/Philip Bliss*

Chorus 1

It is well with my soul It is well It is well with my soul
Verse 1

When peace like a river attendeth my way
When sorrows like sea billows roll
Whatever my lot Thou hast taught me to say
It is well It is well with my soul

Verse 2

Tho' Satan should buffet tho' trials should come
Let this blest assurance control that Christ has regarded
My helpless estate and hath shed His own blood for my soul

Verse 3

My sin O the bliss of this glorious tho't
My sin not in part but the whole is nailed to the cross
And I bear it no more Praise the Lord
Praise the Lord O my soul

Verse 4

And Lord haste the day when my faith shall be sight
The clouds be rolled back as a scroll
The trump shall resound and the Lord shall descend
Even so it is well with my soul

Holy Ground - Geron Davis

We are standing on holy ground
And I know that there
Are angels all around
Let us praise Jesus now
We are standing in His presence
On holy ground

Verse 1

As I walked through the door
I sensed His presence
And I knew this was the place
Where love abounds
For this is a temple
Jehovah God abides here
We are standing in His presence
On holy ground

Verse 2

In His presence
There is joy beyond measure
And at His feet
Peace of mind can still be found
If you have a need
I know He has the answer
Reach out and claim it child
You're standing on holy ground

Lyndon Weberg

What A Friend We Have In Jesus-*Charles Converse/Joseph Scriven*

Verse 1
What a Friend we have in Jesus
All our sins and griefs to bear
What a privilege to carry
Ev'rything to God in prayer
O what peace we often forfeit
O what needless pain we bear
All because we do not carry
Ev'rything to God in prayer

Verse 2
Have we trials and temptations
Is there trouble anywhere
We should never be discouraged
Take it to the Lord in prayer
Can we find a friend so faithful
Who will all our sorrows share
Jesus knows our ev'ry weakness
Take it to the Lord in prayer

Verse 3
Are we weak and heavy laden
Cumbered with a load of care
Precious Savior still our Refuge
Take it to the Lord in prayer
Do thy friends despise forsake thee
Take it to the Lord in prayer
In His arms He'll take and shield thee
Thou wilt find a solace there

Sweet Hour Of Prayer - *William Bradbury / William Walford*

Verse 1
Sweet hour of prayer Sweet hour of prayer
That calls me from a world of care
And bids me at my Father's throne
Make all my wants and wishes known
In seasons of distress and grief my soul has often found Relief and oft
escaped the tempter's snare
By Thy return sweet hour of prayer

Verse 2
Sweet hour of prayer Sweet hour of prayer
The joys I feel the bliss I share of those whose anxious Spirits burn with
strong desires for Thy return
With such I hasten to the place
Where God my Savior shows His face
And gladly take my station there
And wait for Thee sweet hour of prayer

Verse 3
Sweet hour of prayer Sweet hour of prayer
Thy wings shall my petition bear to Him whose truth and Faithfulness
engage the waiting soul to bless
And since He bids me seek His face
Believe His word and trust His grace
I'll cast on Him my ev'ry care
And wait for Thee sweet hour of prayer

Because He Lives - *Gloria Gaither / William Gaither*

Chorus

And because He lives I can face tomorrow
Because He lives all fear is gone
Because I know He holds the future
And life is worth the living
Just because He lives

Verse 1
God sent His Son they called Him Jesus
He came to love heal and forgive
He bled and died to buy my pardon
An empty grave is there to prove
My Savior lives

Verse 2
How sweet to hold our newborn baby
And feel the pride and joy he gives
But greater still the calm assurance
This child can face uncertain days
Because Christ lives

Verse 3
And then one day I'll cross that river
I'll fight life's final war with pain
And then as death gives way to vict'ry
I'll see the lights of glory
And I'll know He reigns

He Paid The Debt

He paid a debt He did not owe
I owed a debt I could not pay
I needed someone to wash my sins away
And now I sing a brand new song, "Amazing Grace"
Christ Jesus paid the debt that I could never pay.

BIBLE STORIES

The following are a brief summary of a few Bible stories that have special meaning to me and perhaps to you, the reader. Please look up the stories in the Bible to gain the full meaning. There are hundreds of beautiful stories in the Word of God, so please enjoy these.

The story of Jesus Christ, found in Mathew, Mark, Luke and John (The 4 Gospels)

For centuries the Jewish people sacrificed lambs, goats, and other animals to God to ask for forgiveness for their sins and atonement for their wrong doings.

About two centuries ago, God sent his Son, Jesus, into the world to be the final sacrifice that was needed for the forgiveness of sins for all mankind. John 3:16 says, *"For God so loved the world that He gave His only begotten Son, and whoever believe in Him would not perish but have eternal Life."*

God is love. All man has to do is to ask Jesus Christ into his heart, and believe in Jesus and obey the 10 commandments. Then man will be saved! The date I was saved was October 19, 1982 and my life has been very joyful and peaceful since that date.

The following are the main events of the life of Jesus:

The Birth of Jesus – Luke 2 (Christmas)

The boy Jesus – Luke 2

The miracles, parables, and healings done by Jesus – Luke chapters 3 through 21

The Last Supper – Luke 22

The Crucifixion of Jesus – Luke 23 (Good Friday)

The Resurrection of Jesus – Luke 24 (Easter) (Jesus rose from the dead with victory over Satan, death, and the world.)

The Ascension of Jesus – Luke 24 (Jesus ascended to heaven 40 days after rising from the dead. He promised to return to earth to gather up all His believers who are ready.)

The Rapture of Jesus – I Thessalonians 4:16-18 (Jesus will come from heaven to gather us up to live with Him forever and ever. With the trump of God, the voice of the archangel, and the shout of God! Jesus will descend from heaven and the dead in Christ will rise first, and all of the living who believe in Jesus will be taken up to live with the Lord forever and ever. Comfort each other with these words. Accept Jesus as indicated above, be ready to go, and you will be taken up with the Lord on Rapture Day!)

The Great Commission – Mathew 28:19 *"Go, therefore and make disciples of all the nations, baptizing them in the name of the Father, in the name of the Son, and in the name of the Holy Spirit."* (This is what we are supposed to be doing until the Lord Jesus returns at the Rapture. So, we must do it.)

The Story of the Holy Spirit – Acts 2

10 days after the Ascension of Jesus into heaven, the Holy Spirit came to a room where all the disciples and other believers were gathered. After 10 days of prayers and communing, suddenly there was a sound of a great rushing wind and small flames of fire sat above the head of each believer. They all started to talk in strange languages that could be understood by others in the group. Many other events occurred at the time and you can read about each one in the Bible reading indicated. The coming of the Holy Spirit, 50 days after the Resurrection is often known as the Pentecost.

God sent us a Comforter to help us while Jesus is away from us. The Holy Spirit gives us love, joy, peace, self-control and many wonderful fruits of the Spirit.

One of the first acts of obedience after a person is born again is to be baptized by the Holy Spirit. This is a wonderful event that occurs when a person can feel the Holy Spirit enter him or her; the evidence of being filled is the "Speaking in Tongues"! I can remember when I was baptized in the Holy Spirit, I felt incredibly happy. I laughed with pure joy and spoke in a language that was unfamiliar to me. The holy language of tongues is still with me today.

Both the Baptism of the Holy Spirit and water baptism (by immersion) are great events in the walk with Jesus Christ!

The Conversion of Saul – Acts 9

A man named Saul was a persecutor of Christian people. He was a Jewish man who beat, murdered and mocked Christians wherever he would go. He really hated the followers of Jesus. Saul broke into Christians' homes and destroyed everything. Saul was instructed by Jewish authorities to go to a nearby town where he would get further instructions about destroying Christians. He was traveling along a road called the Damascus Road and suddenly there was a very bright light that shone from heaven and blinded Saul, and drove him to the ground. A voice came from the light and said, "This is Jesus of Nazareth. Why do you persecute Me so? I want you to be a worker for Me. You will be blind for three days and your associates will take you to a certain address in the city and the people in the house will receive you and they will pray for you."

So Saul was led to this place and waited there with a group of Christians who continually prayed for him. You can read the rest in Acts 9.

Saul was renamed Paul, and he became one of the greatest Christians of all time. He wrote 2/3 of the New Testament, which included letters to the Galatians, Ephesians, Colossians and Philippians. There are many fascinating stories about Paul such as being ship-wrecked, and the serpent story. Read them and enjoy.

The story of the jailer and his conversion to Jesus – Acts 16

Paul and Silas had been beaten and thrown into the dungeon part of the jail and put in stocks by the Jewish authorities for witnessing. It was about midnight and the two men were singing and praising God. There was a great earthquake and the jail shook and prison doors swung open. Everyone's shackles were unfastened.

The jailer of the prison was upset because the authorities would be sure to kill him in the morning once they found out. He was about to kill himself when Paul called out, "Sir, do not harm yourself! We are all here, and have not escaped!"

The jailer was so amazed because they were still there. He was trembling and terrified and fell down before Paul and Silas. He brought them out of the dungeon and asked what he would have to do to be saved. Paul explained what to do and the jailer and his whole family were converted.

The jailer was so excited and happy that he and his family became Christians! Praise the Lord! Surely, the angels in heaven all danced and rejoiced that night because the jailer and his family were all saved! What a great story! Read about it entirely in ACTS 16.

The story of Joseph – Genesis 37

Jacob had 12 sons and the second from youngest was Joseph. He was the favorite son of them all. Joseph was 17 years old, and his older brothers hated him because he was his father's favorite and they felt that he lorded it over them.

The older brothers planned to get rid of Joseph by some means. They threw him into a deep pit until deciding what to do with him. God was with Joseph so he was not afraid in the pit. Later, a band of travelers came near and the older brothers sold him to the travelers. Joseph had a coat of many colors his father had made for him and he wore the coat at all times. The brothers took the coat from Joseph, dipped it in animal blood and brought to Jacob. They told their dad Joseph was killed by a wild animal. Jacob believed them.

The band of travelers was heading for Egypt with the teenager. God was with him on the trip to Egypt, and prospered him in that far away country.

An officer of Pharaoh, the captain and chief executioner of the royal guard, bought him. Joseph was a handsome man and Potiphar's wife tried to seduce him. But the young man would not cooperate with her because he loved God and obeyed all the commandments of God. Because of her lies, Joseph was thrown in prison.

No matter what happened to Joseph, God was with him and taught him to be strong in the Lord. The young man continued to prosper, and ended up being the second in command under Pharaoh over all of Egypt.

About this time a severe famine came over the land and this included Israel also. Jacob sent several of his sons to Egypt in search of food. Joseph gave his brothers food without the brothers recognizing him. He told them to take this food back to their family, and if they needed more they were to come again, and to bring the head of the family with them.

Several months passed and Jacob's household needed more food to make it through the famine. This time all Jacob's sons went to Egypt to get the food, Benjamin included. While they were in Egypt this time, Joseph gave his brothers all the food and supplies they needed. He placed the money they had given him in every bag, and Joseph's silver cup into Benjamin's bag. Then Joseph sent his steward after them to ask, "Why have you rewarded evil for good? Why have you stolen the silver cup?" And the cup was found in Benjamin's sack. They all returned to the city.

Joseph revealed himself to his family and forgave his brothers for being mean to him and selling him to the band of travelers. The brothers were astonished at this and Joseph received their apologies and loved all his brothers and sent them back to the land of Canaan to get their father and families. Joseph told his brothers that even though they had done to him what they did; God had meant it for good! The forgiveness and not holding a grudge makes this one of my favorite stories in the Bible.

The Story of Daniel – found in the book of Daniel

Daniel lived in the Old Testament time. He was a man of God who stood for God at all times. The book of Daniel tells many interesting stories and will certainly keep your attention. One such story is entitled "Daniel and the Lion's Den".

Daniel was in a foreign country and had been brought there by those who had captured his homeland. He was a man of God. Daniel and the king of Babylon had become friends.

Being tricked by Daniel's enemies, the king put forth a decree, that nobody should worship any other gods, that everybody should worship him. He stated that anyone caught not obeying his decree would be thrown into the lion's den, to be eaten by the lions.

Of course Daniel would not worship the king because he was a true man of God. The king had to save face. He had his friend Daniel thrown into the lion's den. The next morning he rushed down to the lion's den to check on him. He cried out, "Daniel, servant of the living God, has your God, whom you serve continually, been able to deliver you from the lions?"

The lions had not hurt him at all. And Daniel answered, "O king, live forever! My God sent His angel and shut the lions' mouths, so that they have not hurt me…"

The King had Daniel brought out of the den and there was not a scratch on him. Because of Daniel's witness, the king made another decree, "that all men of my kingdom must tremble and fear before the God of Daniel. For He is the living God, and steadfast forever…"

God had truly protected Daniel that day because of his strong faith. Praise God!

The story of the fiery furnace is also found in the book of Daniel. This is the story where Hebrew children who, by their strong faith in God, were not harmed at all when they were all thrown into a fiery furnace. You must read the book of Daniel to appreciate this story and many others. Daniel is an interpreter of dreams. You will certainly be intrigued as you read these fantastic stories.

The book of Daniel has many prophesies in it about the Last Days that we are in at the current time.

The story of Jonah – found in the book of Jonah

Jonah was a minister of God. God told Jonah that He wanted him to go to Nineveh to preach God's word. Nineveh was a city filled with sin and corruption. God wanted his preacher to go there to help the people of that city turn to Him.

Jonah was full of fear and ran away from God. He boarded a ship to go a different direction, away from Nineveh. While they were sailing, a great storm arose and Jonah ended up being thrown overboard and swallowed by a great fish. He was in the belly of the fish for three days. He repented to God whom he had disobeyed, and told Him how very sorry he was. He also played back his entire life and asked forgiveness for all his sins and wrong doings. He completely emptied out and received a new burst of energy to do God's bidding.

On the third day the great fish vomited Jonah up, and God again told Jonah to go and preach at Nineveh. This time he obeyed, and the people of that city were sorry for their evil ways and cried out to God for forgiveness. Jonah began to witness, and the whole city turned to God. Jonah was so happy and glad that he had repented to God for his wrongs and got back on the side of God! We can do the same thing and repent to God and He will forgive us and we can be back on God's side, winning souls for God!

The story of Job – found in the book of Job

Job was a man who was blameless and upright during Old Testament times, who reverently feared God and shunned evil. There came a day when the angels presented themselves before the Lord, and Satan also came with them. And the Lord said to Satan, "Where did you come from?"

"From going to and fro on the earth and from walking up and down on it," he brazenly said.

And the Lord told Satan, "Look at Job. See what a good man he is!"

Satan argued with Him. "Yea," he said. "That's because You put a hedge around him and take care of him. If this were not so, he'd curse You!"

And the Lord said to Satan, "Behold, all that he has is in your power, but you cannot kill him."

So Satan went forth from the presence of the Lord.

Job began to lose everything such as cattle, other animals and all his possessions, house, even his children and wife and about everything that Job had that was materialistic in nature. Job's plight was a string of bad luck, more than anyone had ever seen before! It had never been so bad for a man who believed in God.

Job's wife told him to "Curse God!" and then she died. Job would not do that. Next Job's health started to go and he was almost ready to die. The story of Job shows him sitting in a pile of ashes with boils all over his body and head. But Job still insisted, "Whether I live or die, I will bless the Lord!"

Job's story is a great story of faith, and exemplifies what we need to do when everything seems to go wrong. If we remain faithful despite devastating and difficult circumstances, God will help us through the hard times. We must hang in there and believe! God will reward us for our faith and will make us prosper if we continue to obey Him. He'll not only help us endure suffering but lead us to restoration. Job later prospered and continued to have strong faith.

The story of the olives – Exodus 27:20, 21

The Hebrew people in the Old Testament were taught from their ancestors how to process olives from the olive trees to make olive oil to burn the lamps in the temple of God.

The process of doing this is as follows: Put a large cloth around the trunk of the olive tree. Beat the trunk of the tree with wooden sticks and only the ripe olives will fall onto the cloth that lies below the tree on the ground.

Gather up the corners of the cloth with all the olives in the middle of what will become a large ball when the corners are all tied together. This ball of olives in the cloth are then dipped in water and allowed to soak for a period of time. The olives in the bag are then put into a device that squeezes the liquid from the olives and the liquid is caught in a large container. There is some straining to remove some of the waste that has made it through the process and the result is 100% pure olive oil to light the lamps in the temple.

This same process is often how we are to find Jesus as follows: We are gathered up by workers in the Kingdom of God and begin to realize that the large hole in our chest may be filled with something good. Jesus purifies us and cleanses us forgives our sins much like the water in the above process does.

Our confession of our sins and repentance to God is like the squeezing operation in the above process with the olives. Our lives may have had divorce, death, recovery from addiction, and physical challenges, but with each of these we overcome with God's help and become closer to Him with each event.

We become like pure oil and are able to light the lamps of other people's heart for knowing Jesus. As Christians we are to be the "Light of the world!"

This analogy between the purification of the olives for oil to light the lamps of the temple is exactly how people are to be purified for Jesus so they may be the light of the world!

The story of the New Heaven and the New Earth –
Revelation 21: 20, 21

This story is actually what is going to happen at the time we are in heaven with God. It is after the defeat of Satan and the White Throne Judgment. There will be a new heaven and a new earth that will be replacing the old heaven and the old earth. All the believers of Jesus will be in the new heaven and we will be there forever and ever and ever! There will be no more tears, no more grief or crying, no more pain, no blindness, no more physical or mental challenges. All the old things will have disappeared and all things will become new! I am looking forward to 20/20 vision, perfect hearing, and no pain in the back or my eyes. There will be no more of the earthly matters but all will be perfectly new and good!

We win! Satan has been defeated and we'll be living in a perfect setting called heaven! Jesus said, "In My Father's house are many mansions. I go to prepare a place for you. When God sends Me, I will come back to gather you up and take you to heaven to dwell in one of those mansions that I have prepared."

Jesus keeps His promises, so He is coming back to take us to the 'mansions in the sky'! I am going to heaven and you can too. Obey and be blessed!

The above 10 stories are just a small sample of all the wonderful stories in the Bible. Read it, and once you get started you will not be able to put it down. God's Word is so exciting; you will really enjoy reading it. It is useful for today's world. It is the Basic Instructions

Before Leaving Earth! Always remember that God is love and He loves you and all humans. All you have to do is to love Him back and you will be with God.

BIBLE VERSES

The final topic of this book will be a list of Bible verses that I carry in my heart, to be able to live during these last days. The following are some verses from my memory bank that have special meaning to me:

1. *For God so loved the world that He gave His only begotten Son, that whosoever believes in Him will not perish but have everlasting life. John 3:16*
2. *Except a man be born again, he cannot enter the Kingdom of heaven. John 3:3*
3. *If you believe in your heart and confess with your mouth that Jesus Christ was born on earth and suffered and died on the Cross and God raised Jesus from the dead, you will be saved. Romans 10:9*
4. *If you are in Christ all the old things pass away and all things have become new. II Corinthians 5:17*
5. *Do not worry about anything; ask God what you need, be thankful for what you have, and God will give you a peace that passes all human understanding. Philippians 4:6, 7*
6. *Trust in the Lord with all your heart. Do not lean on your own understanding. Acknowledge Him in all your ways, and He will direct your path. Proverbs 3:6,*
7. *Be Patient. James 5:6* (works well in the grocery line)
8. *Resist the devil and he will flee. James 4:8*
9. *Be vigilant and sober. The devil walks around like a roaring lion, seeking who he may devour. I Peter 5: 8*

10. *Create in me a clean heart; renew a right spirit in me. Psalm 51:10*

11. *A double minded man is unstable. James 1:8*

12. *You are neither hot nor cold because you are lukewarm, I will spit you out of My mouth. Revelations 3:15*

13. *God is my refuge and strength, a very present help in the time of trouble. Psalm 46:1*

14. *Make a joyful noise unto the Lord, enter His gates with thanksgiving. Psalm 100:1*

15. *God says, "I will save those who love Me and will protect those who acknowledge Me as Lord. Psalm 92:1*

16. *How good it is to give thanks to You oh Lord, to sing in Your honor, oh most high God. Psalm 92:1*

17. *The Lord is my Shepherd, I shall not want. Psalm 23:1*

18. *My Child, do not go with people like that; stay away from them. Proverbs 1:15*

19. *In the beginning, God created the heavens and the earth. Genesis 1:1*

20. *With a shout and with the voice of the archangel and the trump of God, Jesus will second from heaven and the dead in Christ will rise first and those that are living and believe in Jesus will be caught up with the Lord in the air to live with the Lord forever and ever. Comfort each other with these words. II Thessalonians 4:16-18*

21. *Show a gentle attitude toward all. Philippians 4:5*

22. *We can say with confidence, "The Lord is my helper; I will not be afraid. What can anyone do to me?" Hebrews 13:6*

23. *Jesus said Take courage! It is I. Don't be afraid. Mark 6:50*

24. *Pray in the Spirit at all times, with all prayer and supplication. Ephesians 6:8*

25. *The Psalmist said to God, "How sweet are Your words to my taste, sweeter than honey to my mouth!" Psalm 119:103*

26. *Honor the Lord with your substance and with the first fruits of all your produce; then your barns will be filled with plenty. Proverbs 3:9-10*

27. *Bring all the tithes into the storehouse that there may be food in the house, and try Me now, says the Lord of Hosts. If I will*

not open for you the windows of heaven and pour out for you such a blessing that there will not be room enough to receive it. Malachi 3:10

28. So God created man in His own image, in the image of God He created him, male and female He created them. Genesis 1: 27

29. Of course my friends, I really do not think that I have already won the race, but one thing that I do, is to forget what is behind me and do my best to reach to what is ahead. Philippians 3:13

30. The creation of the world, heavens, sun, moon, and everything else. Genesis 1

31. In the beginning the Word already existed; the Word was with God, and the Word was God. John 1:1

32. Jesus pulled me out of the miry clay. He sat me on a solid rock and made me secure. He taught me to sing a new song, a song of praise to our God. Psalm 40:2, 3

33. One does not live by bread alone, but by every word that comes from the mouth of the Lord. Deuteronomy 8:3

34. The sovereign Lord says, "I will remove from them their heart of stone and give them a heart of flesh." Ezekiel 11:19

35. Let your light shine before others, so that they may see your good works and give glory to your Father in heaven. Matthew 5:16

36. Be joyful in hope, patient in affliction, and faithful in prayer. Romans 12:12

37. Be kind and compassionate to one another, forgiving each other, just as in Christ God forgives you. Ephesians 4:32

38. Jesus was filled with pity, and reached and touched the man with the skin disease. Mark 1:41

39. What you say can preserve life or destroy it; so you must accept the consequences of your words. Proverbs 18:21

40. God did not give us a spirit of cowardice, but rather a spirit of power and of love and of self-discipline. II Timothy 1:7

41. Hope deferred makes the heart sick, but a longing fulfilled is a tree of life. Proverbs 13:12

42. *Let us run with perseverance the race that is set before us, looking to Jesus the pioneer and perfecter of our faith. Hebrews 12: 1,2*

43. *Do not be misled. "Bad company corrupts good character." I Corinthians 15:33*

44. *For God alone my soul waits in silence, from Him comes my salvation. Psalm 62: 1*

45. *Serve one another with whatever gift each of you has received. I Peter 4:10*

46. *We are what He has made us, created in Christ Jesus for good works. Ephesians 2:10*

47. *One does not live by bread alone, but by every word that comes from the mouth of the Lord. Deuteronomy 8:3*

48. *Give thanks in all circumstances, for this is the will of God in Christ Jesus for you. Thessalonians 5:18*

49. *Jesus had compassion on the two blind men and touched their eyes. Matthew 20: 34*

50. *Love must be sincere. Hate what is evil. Cling to what is good. Romans 12:9*

51. *Jesus Christ is the same yesterday, today and forever. Hebrews 13:8*

52. *Come unto Me if you are weary and heavy laden and I will give you rest. Matthew 11:28*

53. *Christ's message in all its richness must live in your hearts. Teach and instruct one another with all wisdom. Colossians 3:16, 17*

54. *For it is by God's Grace that you have been saved through faith. Ephesians 2:8*

55. *I am the first and the last says the Lord God Almighty, who is, who was, and who is to come. Revelations 1:8*

56. *The seven stars are the angels of the seven churches and the seven lamp stands are the seven churches. Revelation 1:20*

57. *And so I walk in the presence of the Lord in the world of the living. Psalm 116:9*

58. *My punishment was good for me, because it made me learn Your commands. Psalm 119:71*

59. *At this point I had another vision and saw an open door in heaven. Revelation 4:1*

60. *After that I heard what sounded like a roar of a large crowd of people in heaven, saying, "Praise God! Salvation, glory and power belong to our God! Revelation 19:1*

61. *To have faith is to be sure of the things we hope for, to be certain of the things we cannot see. Hebrews 11:1*

62. *"Sir," the woman said, "You do not have a bucket and the well is deep. Where would You get that life giving Water?" John 4:11*

63. *"Sir," the woman said, "Give me that water!" John 4:15*

64. *Soon after the trouble of those days, the sun will grow dark, the moon will no longer shine, the stars will fall from heaven, the powers in space will be driven from their courses. Then the sign of the Son of Man will appear in the sky, and all the peoples of earth will weep as they see the Son of Man coming on the clouds of heaven with power and great glory. Matthew 24:29, 30*

65. *The great trumpet will sound, and He will send out His angels to the four corners of the earth, and they will gather His chosen people from one end of the world to the other. Matthew 24:31*

66. *All things work together for the good for those that love God. Romans 8:28*

67. *All have sinned and fall short of the glory of God. Romans 3:23*

68. *The Lord said to Paul, "My power is greatest when you are weak. II Corinthians 12:9*

69. *Ask and it will be given to you; search, and you will find; knock, and the door will be open for you. Matthew 7:7*

70. *Contribute to the needs of the saints; extend hospitality to strangers. Romans 12:13*

71. *The Lord was with Joseph and showed him steadfast love. Genesis 39:21*

72. *Jesus said, "Peace I leave with you; My peace I give you. I do not give to you as the world gives. Do not let your hearts be troubled and do not be afraid." John 14:27*

73. *Jesus said to the ruler, "You still lack one thing. Sell everything you have and give to the poor. Then come, follow Me." Luke 18: 22*

74. *My God shall supply all your needs according to His riches in glory by Christ Jesus. Philippians 4:19*

75. *In all these things we are more than conquerors through God who loved us. Romans 8:37*

76. *The psalmist wrote, "In the day of my trouble I call on You, for You will answer me." Psalm 86:7*

77. *When the hour came, Jesus took His place at the table, and the apostles with Him. Luke 22:14*

78. *The psalmist wrote, "It is good for me to draw near to God. I have put my trust in the Lord God, that I may declare all Thy works." Psalm 73:28*

79. *Jesus said, "I am the Vine, you are the branches. Who abides in Me and I in them bear much fruit, because apart from Me you can do nothing." John 15:5*

80. *For we do not wrestle against flesh and blood but against principalities, against powers, against the rulers of darkness of this age, against spiritual hosts of wickedness in the heavenly places. Ephesians 6:12*

81. *The King will answer the righteous. "Truly I tell you, just as you did it to one of the least of these who are members of my family, you did it to Me." Matthew 25:40*

82. *The King will answer, "I was sick and you took care of Me." Matthew 25:36*

83. *Jesus said, "I come that they may have life, and have it abundantly." John 10:10*

84. *When the prodigal was still far off, his father saw him and ran and put his arm around him. Luke 15:20*

85. *Our Father who art in heaven, hallowed be Thy name. Thy Kingdom come; Thy will be done on earth as it is in heaven. Give us this day our daily bread. Forgive us our trespasses as we forgive those who trespass against us. And lead us not into temptation but deliver us from evil. For Thine is the Kingdom, the power and the glory forever and ever. Amen. Matthew 6:9-13*

86. *Now to Him who is able to do exceedingly abundantly above all that we ask or think, according to the power that works in us… Ephesians 3:20*

87. *In everything give thanks; for this is the will of God in Christ Jesus for you. I Thessalonians 5:18*

88. *He brought me to the banqueting house, and His intension toward me was love. Song of Solomon 2:4*

89. *Neither death nor life … will be able to separate us from the love of God. Romans 8:38*

90. *The 9 beatitudes from the Sermon on the Mount. (Here are 3 of them)*

> *Blessed are those who know they are spiritually poor. The Kingdom of heaven belongs to them!*

> *Blessed are those who are humble, they will receive what God has promised!*

> *Blessed are the pure in heart. They will see God.*

(You may read the rest in Matthew 5:3-12)

91. *Oh taste and see that the Lord is Good; happy are those that take refuge in Him. Psalm 34:8*

92. *Jesus said, "Remember, I am with you always, even to the end of the age." Matthew 23:20*

93. *Commit your way to the Lord; trust in Him, and He will act. Psalm 37:*

94. *Pray at all times I Thessalonians 5:17*

95. *May the grace of the Lord Jesus be with you all. Revelation 22:21*

96. *The effective fervent prayer of a righteous man avails much. James 5:16*

97. *…being confident of this very thing, that He who has begun a good work in you will complete it until the day of Jesus Christ. Philippians 1:6*

98. *The joy of the Lord is my strength. Nehemiah 8:9*

99. *The psalmist wrote, "Return, oh Lord, and deliver me. Save me because of Your unfailing love." Psalm 6:4*

100. *Repent, and turn to God so that your sins may be wiped out, that times of refreshing may come from the Lord. Acts 3:1*

101. *And among them there was what looked like a human being, wearing a robe that reached to His feet, and a gold band around His chest. His hair was white as wool or snow and His eyes blazed like fire; His face was the bright shining sun. His feet shone like brass that has been refined and polished, and His voice sounded like roaring waterfalls. Revelation 1:13-14 (the author of this book gives us a glimpse of what God looks like)*

This is the Weberg 101 (mostly Good News Bible version). My favorite Scripture verses. This small group does not even scratch the surface of all the beautiful verses, plus the verses of warning that are in God's Word.

24. THE TEST OF SALVATION

Either you are saved or you are lost! If you're saved, you love Jesus and remember the day you were saved. My salvation date is 10/19/82. To have a personal relationship with Jesus you must desire to improve your conscious contact with Him on an everyday bases. You must pray often, read and study the Bible daily, and worship Jesus together with other Christians. And you must serve Jesus wherever you can, such as witnessing for Him every day. You now may look forward to spending eternal life with Jesus in heaven! He has filled the huge hole in my chest that I once had before giving my life to Jesus! Praise God!

If you are lost, you do not care. You feel unworthy, too busy, do not believe in religion, and feel no good. You need to have Jesus Christ to come into your life, to let the Lord give you fullness and worth, and a heavenly home to look forward to in the future. Surely you are going to die like everyone else, and you need to make a decision where your soul (your mind, will and emotions) is going to spend eternity. Everyone has a soul and it's up to us while we are alive to decide where we want our soul to spend eternity. Our choices are heaven (a wonderful place that Jesus has prepared for believers) or hell (a terrible place of constant fires, gnashing of teeth, and torment with no relief forever and ever). This is a place of total separation from God (God is love), and you will never hear the Word of God again. What a terrible place hell will be for Satan and his angels! This is where non-believers will end up, forever and ever!

It is God's will that no one should perish because God is love, and He loves you and all people. It's easy to choose heaven as your destination, that final home, by saying the sinner's prayer. Here is a form of the prayer, once again.

Dear Jesus, come into my heart right now. Forgive all my sins that I have ever committed. Remove them from me as far as the east is from the west. Create in me a clean heart, that I may live for You the rest of my earthly life. I thank You for saving my soul today. Now I will spend eternity with You (in heaven). I look forward to serving You from this point in my life in witnessing to others so that they too may have salvation. I pray, dear Jesus, that You will live in me the rest of my days. Thank You oh Lord, for saving me today!

If you say this prayer today and mean it, this date is your salvation date to remember permanently. You'll need to get a Bible and start reading the book of John in the New Testament. Find a full gospel Assembly of God type church and begin attending. You will learn more about Jesus. Meet the pastor of the church and tell him you are a new convert. Have him teach you how to pray. There are different groups at church that you can join to become stronger in your walk with God.

Thank you for being a fellow worker with me in the Kingdom of God. You now have heaven to look forward to after your earthly life is complete. The angels in heaven are dancing and rejoicing about you joining Jesus.

There is no person that cannot bond with Jesus. Look at Saul whom we discussed earlier. As an ex-gambler, joining Jesus is a 'lock' and it is the most important decision that I'll ever make. We are in the last days before Jesus comes, so I'm glad to be a Christian and am very happy that you have decided to be a Christian too.

How do I know it's close to the Rapture? The Bible tells us so. Wars, rumors of war, earthquakes, people living in sexual sin, etc. The world news last evening had these topics as headlines:

1. Swine flu Epidemic Spreads
2. Iran Sends up Another Nuclear Warhead
3. Brutal Beating of a 16 Year Old Boy outside of a School in South Chicago
4. Tsunami Shakes Samoa and American Samoa with many Deaths and Injuries

These stories indicate that 'the Rapture' is getting closer and that all of these events are in line for the Battle of Armageddon that is mentioned in the Bible. Situations are lining up, just as God has told us in His Word.

Remember that Satan is the prince of the earth and his mission is to kill, steal and destroy. This is why our news is as it is. It is a report of Satan's work on earth today. Just be saved, and do not let this world and its events bother you. Do not miss the Rapture!

I am heading to church on this Wednesday evening to worship Jesus and to be with my Christian friends. Please come too. The reason I live is to worship Jesus! It's the reason I exist. Please join me. Praise God!

THE LORD JESUS CHRIST IS COMING SOON!

THE LORD JESUS WILL RETURN AT ANY TIME. OUR COUNTRY IS BECOMING VERY CORRUPT AND FILLED WITH GREED, DISHONESTY, LYING, AND TOTAL SELF-RELIANCE. SATAN IS HAVING A FIELD DAY AT THIS TIME! THESE LAST DAYS ARE AS THE DAYS OF NOAH BEFORE THE FLOOD WHERE GOD WIPED OUT ALL THE UNFAITHFUL AND SAVED ONLY NOAH AND HIS FAMILY ON THE ARK. THE RAPTURE IS COMING NOW JUST AS THE FLOOD CAME. WE MUST BE READY. IF YOU ARE SAVED NOW (HAVE A NEW HEART AND THE HOLY SPIRIT) THEN YOU WILL GO WITH THE LORD JESUS IN THE RAPTURE. IF NOT YOU WILL BE LEFT BEHIND IN THE TRIBULATION PERIOD. GOD'S WORD SAYS THAT WE SHOULD LOOK FOR WARS AND RUMORS OF WARS, EARTHQUAKES MORE FREQUENTLY, AND PEOPLE GOING AWAY FROM GOD, MUCH IMMORALITY, AND OTHER SIGNS. THE LORD IS COMING SOON! HE WILL COME WITH A SHOUT! WITH THE VOICE OF THE ARCHANGEL! AND WITH THE TRUMP OF GOD! JESUS HIMSELF WILL DESCEND FROM HEAVEN AND THE DEAD IN CHRIST WILL RISE FIRST, THOSE WHO ARE LIVING AND BELIEVE IN THE LORD WILL BE CAUGHT UP IN THE AIR TO LIVE WITH THE LORD JESUS IN HEAVEN FOR EVER AND EVER! WE ARE TO COMFORT EACH OTHER WITH THESE THOUGHTS. I THESSALONIANS 4: 16-18.

I PRAY THAT READERS OF THIS BOOK WILL BE SAVED AND LIVE IN HEAVEN FOREVER! AND HAVE A WIN! WIN! STORY TOO!